I mean as a Marker of
Intersubjective Adjustment

Hituzi Linguistics in English

No. 4	*A Historical Study of Referent Honorifics in Japanese*	Takashi Nagata
No. 5	*Communicating Skills of Intention*	Tsutomu Sakamoto
No. 6	*A Pragmatic Approach to the Generation and Gender Gap in Japanese Politeness Strategies*	Toshihiko Suzuki
No. 7	*Japanese Women's Listening Behavior in Face-to-face Conversation*	Sachie Miyazaki
No. 8	*An Enterprise in the Cognitive Science of Language*	Tetsuya Sano et al.
No. 9	*Syntactic Structure and Silence*	Hisao Tokizaki
No. 10	*The Development of the Nominal Plural Forms in Early Middle English*	Ryuichi Hotta
No. 11	*Chunking and Instruction*	Takayuki Nakamori
No. 12	*Detecting and Sharing Perspectives Using Causals in Japanese*	Ryoko Uno
No. 13	*Discourse Representation of Temporal Relations in the So-Called Head-Internal Relatives*	Kuniyoshi Ishikawa
No. 14	*Features and Roles of Filled Pauses in Speech Communication*	Michiko Watanabe
No. 15	*Japanese Loanword Phonology*	Masahiko Mutsukawa
No. 16	*Derivational Linearization at the Syntax-Prosody Interface*	Kayono Shiobara
No. 17	*Polysemy and Compositionality*	Tatsuya Isono
No. 18	*fMRI Study of Japanese Phrasal Segmentation*	Hideki Oshima
No. 19	*Typological Studies on Languages in Thailand and Japan*	Tadao Miyamoto et al.
No. 20	*Repetition, Regularity, Redundancy*	Yasuyo Moriya
No. 21	*A Cognitive Pragmatic Analysis of Nominal Tautologies*	Naoko Yamamoto
No. 22	*A Contrastive Study of Responsibility for Understanding Utterances between Japanese and Korean*	Sumi Yoon
No. 23	*On Peripheries*	Anna Cardinaletti et al.
No. 24	*Metaphor of Emotions in English*	Ayako Omori
No. 25	*A Comparative Study of Compound Words*	Makiko Mukai
No. 26	*Grammatical Variation of Pronouns in Nineteenth-Century English Novels*	Masami Nakayama
No. 27	*I mean as a Marker of Intersubjective Adjustment*	Takashi Kobayashi

Hituzi Linguistics in English

27

Takashi Kobayashi

—

I mean as a Marker of Intersubjective Adjustment

—

A Cognitive Linguistic Approach

HITUZI
SYOBO

Copyright © Takashi Kobayashi 2018
First published 2018

Author: Takashi Kobayashi

All rights reserved. Except for the quotation of short passages for the purposes of criticism and review, no part of this publication may be reproduced, stored in a retrieval system, or transmitted in any form or by any means, electronic, mechanical, photocopying, recording or otherwise, without the written prior permission of the publisher.

In case of photocopying and electronic copying and retrieval from network personally, permission will be given on receipts of payment and making inquiries. For details please contact us through e-mail. Our e-mail address is given below.

Hituzi Syobo Publishing

Yamato bldg. 2f, 2-1-2 Sengoku
   Bunkyo-ku Tokyo, Japan 112-0011
Telephone: +81-3-5319-4916
Facsimile: +81-3-5319-4917
e-mail: toiawase@hituzi.co.jp
http://www.hituzi.co.jp/
postal transfer: 00120-8-142852

ISBN978-4-89476-902-1
Printed in Japan

Acknowledgements

First and foremost, I would like to express my deepest gratitude to Yoshihisa Nakamura; he has inspired me and motivated me to study language more deeply, especially the areas of pragmatics and cognitive linguistics. During my research, he was responsible for advising me, sometimes for several hours, and providing constructive comments every time I digressed and headed into erratic and irrational directions. Every moment with him provided a new source for this work; tips that improved my thinking were scattered in serious talks before and after presentations as well as in casual talks over lunch and dinner, lectures, and speeches. I also express my gratitude to Yuko Horita for her thoughtful attention and honest but heart-warming comments on not only my research but also my life. It is because of Professor Nakamura and Professor Horita that I have been able to complete this book.

I am also grateful to professors from other departments at Kanazawa University for their continuous support: Yoshinori Nishijima, Wataru Takei, and Yoshiharu Takeuchi. Discussions with those who have already graduated from, and are still studying at the graduate school of Kanazawa University have been fundamental to my analysis: Takeshi Koguma, Sadashi Mori, Qu Li, Mizue Matsumoto, Kosuke Matsumoto, Rie Mukai, Hiromi Nakatani, Takafumi Marui, Atsushi Hirota, and Akira Takashima. Kanazawa University provided a notable research support through the Cultural Resource Manager Training Program, for which I was selected in 2012; its grant covered most of my research expenses during the 22 days I spent for research in Boston, U.S.A. Without the speech data collected at Tufts University through this program, I would have been unable to provide the reliable data on which this dissertation is based. Therefore, I am indebted to the professors at Tufts University, Hosea Hirata, Charles Inouye, Kiyomi Kagawa, Shiori Koizumi, Kiyoko Morita, and her husband, who gave me the opportunity to collect the speech data. I also want to thank Tufts graduates Jeffery Goldman, Joseph Gummar, Patrick Lee, Alexander Michaelson, and Nathan Paine, and Richard Keefe and Ryan

Standage, English teachers at Hokkoku English Conversation College, for their insightful comments on my study as native speakers of English. I would also like to express my gratitude to the following scholars, whose helpful comments on my presentations and papers were greatly beneficial: Hideo Hamada, Yasuaki Ishizaki, Akira Machida, Hiroyuki Miyashita, Kunie Miyaura, Kojiro Nabeshima, Lawrence Schourup, Toshihiro Tamura, Hiroaki Tanaka, Masako Tsuzuki, Satoshi Uehara, and Masaaki Yamanashi. I wish particularly to thank my colleague Yoshimi Kawabata for her huge support at Ishikawa National Institution of Technology, Ishikawa College.

I gratefully acknowledge the financial support of the Japan Society for the Promotion of Science in turning my dissertation into a book. I am also grateful to editorial support (and their tolerance) from the staff at publisher Hituzi Shobo, especially Takasi Moriwaki, Eri Ebisawa, Sino Suzuki and Nao Aikawa.

My heartfelt gratitude goes to my parents, Minoru and Shizuko, who have supported me with their love and encouragement throughout my graduate studies. Finally, a special word of thanks to my loving wife, Ikumi, who has supported me in numerous ways.

Takashi Kobayashi

Contents

Acknowledgements		V
List of Figures		XI
List of Tables		XIII
List of Abbreviations		XIV
Transcription Conventions		XV

CHAPTER 1
Introduction

1.1	Aims of the Study	1
1.2	Outline of the Book	5

CHAPTER 2
Overview of the Discourse Marker *I mean*

2.1	Introduction	7
2.2	Characteristics of the Usages of *I mean*	7
2.3	Dominant Occurrences	11

CHAPTER 3
Background

3.1	Introduction	15
3.2	Chronological Change	16
3.3	Previous Studies and Their Empirical Problems	20
3.3.1	Schiffrin (1987)	20
3.3.2	Fox Tree and Schrock (2002)	24
3.3.3	Imo (2005)	25

3.3.4	Brinton (2008)	28
3.3.5	Other Previous Studies	30
3.4	Summary	31

CHAPTER 4
A Pragmatic Account of *I mean*

4.1	Introduction	35
4.2	Analysis from Grice's Conversational Maxims	36
4.2.1	Grice's Cooperative Principle and the Four Maxims	36
4.2.2	*I mean* at the What-Is-Said Level	38
4.2.3	*I mean* at the Implicature Level	39
4.3	Analysis from Politeness Theory	43
4.3.1	Politeness Theory	44
4.3.2	*I mean* to Save Hearer's Negative Face	46
4.3.3	*I mean* to Save Speaker's and Hearer's Positive Face	48
4.4	Summary	50

CHAPTER 5
A Cognitive Linguistic Account of *I mean*

5.1	Introduction	53
5.2	The Basic Tenet of Cognitive Linguistics	54
5.3	Relevant Notions of Cognitive Linguistics	55
5.3.1	Profiling	55
5.3.2	Construal	56
5.3.3	Reference Point Relationship	56
5.3.4	Grounding	57
5.3.5	Intersubjectivity	58
5.3.6	Current Discourse Space	61
5.3.7	Anchoring Structure	66
5.4	Analysis from Cognitive Linguistics	68
5.4.1	On Semantic and Pragmatic Functions	68
5.4.1.1	Subjectification in Verhagen (2005, 2007)	68
5.4.1.1.1	Objective Construal Configuration I: Original Meanings	68

5.4.1.1.2	Objective Construal Configuration II: The What-Is-Said Level	69
5.4.1.1.3	Subjective Construal Configuration I: The Implicature Level	70
5.4.1.1.4	Subjective Construal Configuration II: The Face Level	72
5.4.1.1.5	Subjective Construal Configuration III: The Face and Speech Management Levels	73
5.4.1.1.6	Usages of *I mean* and Subjectification	75
5.4.1.2	Problems with the Analysis in Terms of Intersubjectivity (Verhagen 2005, 2007)	76
5.4.1.3	*I mean* at Different Levels of CDS	77
5.4.1.3.1	The Effective Level	77
5.4.1.3.2	The Discursive Level	78
5.4.1.3.3	The Face Level	79
5.4.1.3.4	The Speech Management Level	80
5.4.1.3.5	The Usages of *I mean* outside the Scope of CDS	81
5.4.1.3.6	A New Model of CDS with Multiple Phases	82
5.4.2	Relationships between the Usages of *I mean*	86
5.4.3	On Positions in Discourse	87
5.4.3.1	*I mean* as a Part of the Core: Original Meanings	88
5.4.3.2	*I mean* as a Discursive Anchor: The Effective and Discursive Levels	89
5.4.3.3	*I mean* as a Discursive Anchor: The Speech Management Level	90
5.4.3.4	Clause Internal *I mean* as a Parenthetical Insertion	91
5.5	Implications of the Cognitive Linguistic Account of Other Discourse Markers	92
5.6	Summary	93

CHAPTER 6

I mean as a Marker of Intersubjective Adjustment

97

References 99
Index 105

List of Figures

Figure 3.1:	Correlated paths of directionality in semantic change	16
Figure 3.2:	Syntactic development of pragmatic markers	17
Figure 3.3:	A discourse model	20
Figure 3.4:	Planes of talk on which markers function	22
Figure 3.5:	Network of constructions related to *I mean*	28
Figure 5.1:	The formation of integrated conceptualization	54
Figure 5.2:	The cognitive linguistic model of the relationship between semantics and pragmatics	55
Figure 5.3:	Profile and base	55
Figure 5.4:	Reference point relationship	57
Figure 5.5:	Nominal/clausal grounding	58
Figure 5.6:	The basic construal configuration	58
Figure 5.7:	Maximally objective construal configuration	59
Figure 5.8:	Highly subjective construal configuration	59
Figure 5.9:	*I think* as a matrix clause	60
Figure 5.10:	*I think* as an epistemic marker	60
Figure 5.11:	CDS	62
Figure 5.12:	Viewing frame	63
Figure 5.13:	*Uh* as a filler	63
Figure 5.14:	Spanish second person pronoun *tu*	64
Figure 5.15:	Levels of CDS related to *because*	66
Figure 5.16:	Anchoring structure	67
Figure 5.17:	Original meanings of *I mean*	69
Figure 5.18:	*I mean* at the what-is-said level	70
Figure 5.19:	*I mean* at the implicature level	72
Figure 5.20:	*I mean* at the face level and speech management levels	75
Figure 5.21:	The usages of *I mean* as a process of subjectification	76
Figure 5.22:	*I mean* at the effective level	78
Figure 5.23:	*I mean* at the discursive level	79
Figure 5.24:	*I mean* at the face level	80
Figure 5.25:	*I mean* at the speech management level	81
Figure 5.26:	A new CDS: *I mean* at the discursive level	83
Figure 5.27:	A new CDS: *I mean* at the face level	85
Figure 5.28:	The relationships between the usages of *I mean*	86
Figure 5.29:	Original meaning of *I mean* (i)	88
Figure 5.30:	Original meaning of *I mean* (ii)	89
Figure 5.31:	Original meaning of *I mean* (iii)	89
Figure 5.32:	*I mean* at the effective level	90

Figure 5.33: *I mean* at the discursive level   90
Figure 5.34: *I think* as a parenthetical insertion   91
Figure 5.35: Positions of *I mean*   96

List of Tables

Table 2.1: Functions and positions of *I mean* — 11
Table 2.2: Age of informants — 12
Table 2.3: Language background of informants — 12
Table 2.4: Token frequency of discourse markers in CRMTP data — 12
Table 2.5: Frequency of markers (average number of tokens per minute) in conversations between pairs of strangers and pairs of friends — 13
Table 2.6: Type frequency of *I mean* in CRMTP data — 13
Table 3.1: The semantic development of *I mean* — 18
Table 3.2: The constructional schema of the *I mean* construction — 26
Table 3.3: The constructional schemas of the discourse marker construction and the complement-taking verb *to mean* construction — 27
Table 4.1: The usages of *I mean* at the what-is-said level and implicature level — 43
Table 4.2: The relationship between the speech-act type and threats to face — 46
Table 4.3: Token frequency of *(I'm) Sorry I mean* in PDE corpora — 49
Table 4.4: A pragmatic account of the motivation for using *I mean* — 50
Table 5.1: Levels of CDS related to *because* — 66

List of Abbreviations

C:	Conceptualizer	NF:	Negative Face
CDS:	Current Discourse Space	PCI:	Particularized Conversational Implicature
CG:	Cognitive Grammar		
CP:	Cooperative Principle	PDE:	Present-day English
FTAs:	Face Threatening Acts	PF:	Positive Face
GCI:	Generalized Conversational Implicature	S:	Speaker
		TRP:	Transition Relevance Point
H:	Hearer	$C_{\exists}$:	Existential Core
IU:	Intonation Unit	$V_{\exists}$:	Existential Verb
MS:	Mental Space	+>:	Conversationally Implicate

Transcription Conventions

,	Continuing Intonation
...	Noticeable Pause or Break
-	Self-Interruption with Glottal Stop
:	Lengthened Syllable
CAPITAL LETTERS	Emphatic Stress
[	Starting Point of Overlap of Speech
]	Ending Point of Overlap of Speech
=	Continuing Speech
hhh	Laughter

CHAPTER 1
Introduction

1.1 Aims of the Study

This whole book is dedicated to not only the multiple meanings of a single expression, *I mean*, but also to the cognitive process behind its use. Why *I mean*? Our interest is not only in the primitive issue of "meaning of meaning" (cf. Ogden and Richards 1923), but also the various realizations of *I mean* in English conversations. This book aims to show that what motivates speakers to use *I mean* can be ascribed to the interaction between the speaker and hearer at various levels of discourse, which we call "intersubjectivity." This aspect of *I mean* cannot be irreducible to the two original meanings of the verb *mean*: to *signify* and *intend* (cf. Schiffrin 1987).

Since Schiffrin (1987: 310) called *I mean* a marker of "speaker-orientation," scholars have paid more attention to how speakers modify the propositional information before and after the expression than to the reason why it is used, or to the interaction between the speaker and hearer. In previous studies, various discourse functions of *I mean* have been presented, such as repair, causal meaning, explication, and interpersonal (e.g., Schiffrin 1987; Tanaka and Ishizaki 1994; Fox Tree and Schrock 2002; Takahara, Hayashi, and Hayashi 2002; Imo 2005; Brinton 2008; Matsui 2009). These studies contributed to the clarification of when and how *I mean* is used in discourse. The following examples show the functions of repair, causal meaning, and explication respectively.

(1) I haven't been to Florida. *I mean*, I have.   (CRMTP 13)[1]
(2) I never transfer if you don't have to. *I mean*, it's just such a pain in the ass. Like you have to write so many essays and stuff.   (CRMTP 4)
(3) a. He says, "Oh, I wish you could come with me!"
     b. And I said—I was very pro- proper and prim!
     c. And I said, "Oh, I couldn't go away with you."

    d. And he says, "*I mean* let's get married!"
    e. And I said, "Oh, okay!"   (Schiffrin 1987: 297)

In (1), the phrase *I haven't* is repaired with *I have*. When the speaker is asked if he has been to Florida, he first answers that he has never been before realizing that he actually has. In the repair uses, the speaker corrects the information from his own preceding utterance. The speaker and hearer in (2) are university students, and the former rejects the idea of transferring to another school. The information after *I mean* illustrates the reason why transferring is so frustrating for him. *I mean* in this usage can be paraphrased as *because* or *I'm saying this because* (Brinton 2008: 116). In example (3), a re-enacted proposal scene, the speaker of the entire utterance misunderstood what was implied, hence after *I mean*, he explicitly shows his intention (= (d)). Whereas many other tokens represent the usage of "explication," no other examples show the speaker's misunderstanding of what was said and implied as clearly as (3); thus, it repeatedly appears in this paper.

Although the labels on the functions help us understand how *I mean* works to achieve the "local coherence" of talk (Schiffrin 1987: 21–29), they do not show what motivates the speaker to use *I mean* in a specific context, nor how such functions relate to each other.

In this study, using a cognitive linguistic framework and focusing on the interaction between the speaker and hearer rather than the speaker and propositional information, we claim that *I mean* is a marker for intersubjective adjustment in the sense that the speaker uses it when noticing that the hearer is paying attention to something different from the speaker. The process of cognition, hidden behind the use and the labels of *I mean*, is based on the basic cognitive abilities of specificity, reference point, and intersubjectivity.

Only cognitive linguistics enables us to describe both the core meaning of *I mean* and its extensions in a uniform manner. This theory considers linguistic meaning as conceptualization, meaning it reflects the mental operations of how we perceive the world (Langacker 2008: 4). The question of why we use an expression can also be ascribed to basic cognitive abilities such as abstraction (schematization), figure/ground organization, conceptual reification, and image schemas and metaphor (Langacker 1999: 2–3). For the description of the expression *I mean*, the notions of specificity, reference-point, and intersubjectivity are fundamental. As we will see in Chapter 2, *I mean* has various usages from reference to propositional content and speaker intention to saving the speaker's face to turn-taking. The fact that some usages of *I mean* reflect the original meaning of the verb *mean* while the others do not tends to lead to discussion of whether *I mean* is meaningful or meaningless—in other words, whether or not it has truth-conditional meaning (cf. Schourup 1999: 242–243) and, hence, which is the more appropriate approach, semantics or pragmatics? However, cognitive grammar (CG) does not concern itself with these issues. In CG, multiple meanings in polysemy are treated as a network in which prototypical, specific, schematic meanings are related to each other in some fashion (Langacker 1999: 124–128), and a strict boundary between semantics and pragmatics is not presupposed (Langacker 2008: 40). In this study, the usages of *I mean* will be classified in terms of the motivation for its use and considered to form a gradation, which will be mapped onto a network. In short, it represents a series of cognitive processes and levels of discourse that both distinguish and link usages.

In terms of the pragmatic and cognitive linguistic theories especially designed to describe phenomena in human conversation, the most critical factors in the principle of using *I mean* are Grice's Conversational Maxims, Politeness Theory,[2] and the notion of "intersubjectivity." From a pragmatic perspective, the reasons for using *I mean* can be categorized as follows:

1. The speaker realizes that he has not followed Grice's Maxims in "what is said" in his previous utterance (what-is-said level),
2. the speaker realizes that he has not followed Grice's Maxims in the implicature of his previous utterance (implicature level),
3. the speaker realizes that he has threatened the addressee's negative face (NF) (face level), or
4. the speaker wants to save his own positive face (PF) (however, this can be applied to all usages of *I mean*).[3]

The replacement of information by *I mean* is triggered either by incorrectness or discomfort in the previous utterance that the speaker notices or instantly realizes during speech. Grice's Maxims and Brown & Levinson's Politeness Theory provide a rational explanation for the motivation for using I mean: the incorrectness or discomfort in what the speaker says and implicates, and also when the speaker threatens the hearer's face. However, neither Grice's Maxims nor Politeness Theory can account for the usage of *I mean* in cases when the speaker and hearer fail to jointly attend to the same entity. Roughly speaking, Grice's account for the generation of implicature is based on his Cooperative Principle (CP); it is natural for both the speaker and hearer to think that the speaker made a certain implication (expression p entails an implicature q),[4] in which both interlocutors paid attention to the same entity. Politeness Theory then suggests an explanation for why the speaker violates the maxims. However, both pragmatic accounts fail to explain the motivation for using *I mean* when the speaker and the hearer attend to the different entities. This is the reason cognitive linguistic accounts, particularly notions of intersubjectivity and

Current Discourse Space (CDS), are necessary.

The term "intersubjectivity" can be applied to any kind of interaction between the speaker and hearer, with the proviso that the speaker's intention to elicit the interaction must be involved. The intersubjective interactions are realized in different levels of discourse: physical, epistemic, discursive, and social. Assuming Verhagen's term of "intersubjectivity" (Verhagen 2005, 2007), the usage of *I mean* involves two types of construal: "objective construal configuration," in which the speaker refers to propositional content; and "subjective construal configuration," in which the speaker's use is attributed to the hearer's misunderstanding of the speaker. The usages of *I mean* can be treated as a gradient shift in profile from objective to subjective elements. Verhagen's idea of intersubjectivity alone, however, would not account for all the inevitable motivations for using *I mean*, such as face-saving and turn-taking.

To support Verhagen's intersubjectivity, we must employ CDS, Langacker's new description for dynamically evolving conceptualization in discourse. Including not only objective contents, profile, and various types of contexts but also joint attention, face-saving, turn-taking, and other intersubjective notions, CDS covers all usages of *I mean*. Langacker's CDS, together with Verhagen's intersubjectivity, provide the theoretical background for the motivation of using *I mean*:

> The speaker uses *I mean* to achieve intersubjective adjustment (functioning at the interaction portion of the ground) specifically to draw joint attention at different levels of discourse:
> - The propositional content level (equal to the effective level),
> - The implicature/speech-act level (equal to discursive level),
> - The face level, and
> - The turn level (equal to the speech management level).

At each level, *I mean* signals the speaker and hearer to direct their attention to different entities, also signaling the speaker's aim to direct it to the same one. This is the very cognitive process of what I call "intersubjective adjustment." More specifically, by *I mean*, the speaker directs the hearer's attention to the objective content (required to be corrected) at the propositional content level, (unconveyed) implicature and (misfired) speech act at the implicature/speech-act level, (threatened) face at the face level, and (favorable) turn at the speech management level. Although CDS, as a conversation model in CG, includes pragmatic perspectives and seems to account for every usage of *I mean*, the current CDS in Langacker (2001, 2008) is still not sufficiently dynamic to describe the complicated cognitive process of *I mean*. To solve the issue of dynamicity, a new style of CDS with multiple phases will be proposed at the end of this study.

1.2 Outline of the Book

The work is organized as follows. General characteristics and notable usages of *I mean* will be shown in Chapter 2. Following this chapter, the study of the diachronic change in *I mean* (Brinton 2008) will be introduced to trace its historical semantic and syntactic development. I will also review previous studies and indicate their critical problems. In Chapter 4, the motivations for using *I mean* will be analyzed in terms of pragmatic theories, namely Grice's Maxims and Brown and Levinson's Politeness Theory. In Chapter 5, after identifying a few examples of *I mean* that do not seem to be well explained by pragmatic theories, the semantic/pragmatic as well as structural aspects of *I mean* will be analyzed in terms of the notions of intersubjectivity and CDS in CG. At the end of this chapter, I argue that analysis based on cognitive linguistic theories is fairly applicable to other discourse markers such as *you know* and *like*. The conclusions are demonstrated in Chapter 6.

Notes
1 CRMTP stands for data collected in Cultural Resource Manager Training Program 2012, organized by Kanazawa University (cf. Kobayashi 2013). Also, see section 2.3.
2 Politeness Theory, which I refer to in this book, is based on the model in Brown and Levinson (1987).
3 The first three factors concern the speaker's realization of the necessity of using *I mean* to replace the information before *I mean* (for the sake of the hearer), while the fourth one concerns the speaker's own desires.
4 The process of how the speaker generates an implicature and how the hearer interprets it is described as follows (Grice 1975: 50):
   A general pattern for the working out of a conversational implicature might be given as follows: 'He has said that *p*; there is no reason to suppose that he is not observing the maxims, or at least the CP; he could not be doing this unless he thought that *q*; he knows (and knows that I know that he knows) that I can see that the supposition that he thinks that *q* is required; he has done nothing to stop me thinking that *q*; he intends me to think, or is at least willing to allow me to think, that *q*; and so he has implicated that *q*.'

CHAPTER 2

Overview of the Discourse Marker *I mean*

2.1 Introduction

Discourse markers are so-called function words with particular pragmatic functions. Through diachronic change, discourse markers lose the truth-conditional meaning of their compositional elements and gain pragmatic functions instead. Schiffrin (1987: 31) defines discourse markers as *sequentially dependent elements which bracket units of talk*. She defines such markers based on "units of talk," rather than easily definable syntactic or phonological units. This enables the term "unit" to remain open to a variety of discourse parts. As there are numerous levels in discourse, there should be various degrees to how original meanings reflect on discourse markers (cf. ibid. 315–322). As shown below, the usages of *I mean* include those referring to propositional content[1] and implicature (wherein components' meanings are somehow affected) as well as the one for the purpose of saving the hearer's face and taking a turn in conversation.

2.2 Characteristics of the Usages of *I mean*

The typical usage of *I mean* (which is the most frequent one in Tanaka and Ishizaki 1994 and also in my data from the Cultural Resource Manager Training Program, CRMTP see Table 2.1 and 2.5.) is to correct/rephrase propositional content or to add relevant information to compensate for stammering or a shortage of information before *I mean*.

(4) I haven't been to Florida. *I mean*, I have. (= (1))
(5) And so with my advisor we decided that I'm going to take chemistry and so I have to have either two chem, or two philosophy- *I mean* two physics courses for a bio major. (CRMTP 6)

In the examples above, the incorrect propositional contents *haven't been* and *philosophy* are replaced with what the speaker believes to be true.

(6) 01 M: So...but you speak Japanese, right?
    02 L: Somewhat. *I mean*, I'm like, I can do conversation- I'm
    03   conversationally fluent but like you know, there's all those
    04   like levels of speech. My mom is like, it's better you don't.
                                                                    (CRMTP 3)

Unlike the use of *I mean* in (4) and (5) to correct information, the speaker in (6) uses *I mean* to add extra information, namely information qualifying that she speaks some Japanese, but not perfectly. In other words, the speaker adds information to insufficient propositional content. While the speaker refers to propositional content in the examples above, in the examples below, the speaker uses *I mean* to refer to his intention.

(7) 01 L: Do you have a car?
    02 T: I mean like my family has two cars.
    03 L: Okay but not here.
    04 T: *I mean*, sophomores aren't even allowed to have cars here,
    05   are they?   (CRMTP 9)

The interlocutors L and T in (7) both go to the same university; L wants to know if T has a car or not. The participants of the conversation know that T's house is located a 40-minute drive away from the university, and he often goes back to see his mother. T does not own a car but can use a car anytime he wants. As seen in lines 04–05, T thinks that second-year students are not permitted to park on campus. T's reference to his family in line 02 implicitly shows that he does not have a car on campus, as it is not allowed, but he drives a car his family owns. In 03, L confirms his intended meaning (i.e., he does not have a car). Thereafter, in 04–05, T refers to what he had implied by adducing the reason for his not having a car on campus. This process is, in other words, an adjustment between what the speaker and hearer have in mind.

Considering the reasons a speaker uses *I mean*, classification of usages needs to be done carefully as there are few signs revealing the speaker's purpose in conversations. For example, when you take an *I mean* to be classified as traditional turn-keeping or filler, whether the speaker uses *I mean* to keep turn of the conversation, to add information, or to show his intention, all depends on numerous factors, such as intonation, pauses, and various kinds of contexts. Most examples are not unambiguously classifiable into any one category. Example (8) below shows one such example, in which the speaker intends to take a turn in the conversation.

(8) 01 A: Yeah, but he says homie and he's like- he clarified to me just
    02   like a homie is very different from a friend. It's like it's
    03   someone who knows, who gets it. Do you know what I mean?
    04   When I say that like,
    05 B: Not many peo- er, I'm from Silicon Valley so we don't say
    06   homie =
    07 A: Yeah.
    08 B: = like that.
    09 A: Yeah, but like.
    10 B: *I mean*, there ⎡ may be   couple of people. ⎤
    11 A: ⎣ Do you understand,   ⎦ do you
    12   understand what I mean? Like, he, he clarified like it's not a
    13   friend, it's someone who knows. Like someone who gets it,
    14   someone who is one like on your level like that's my homie
    15   like, this dude is a home like I don't know how to explain…
    16 B: It's kinda bro.   (CRMTP 16)

In (8), the interlocutors are speaking of the word *homie*. Although A believes that *homie* is prevalent in California, B from California denies it. In lines 01–04, A refers to a friend from California who gave him a definition of the word, and in lines 05–06, B says he personally does not use it. Persisting in expounding what he heard from his friend, A does not withdraw his assertion. A's persistency and B's high pitch when saying *I mean* lead to the following conclusion: Buses *I mean* in line 10 so as to have a turn in the conversation or even to end the discussion.

Although this usage has low token frequency, in some usages of *I mean*, the speaker shows consideration for others and attempts to anticipate what the hearer has in mind. In (9), student A speaks of an interview to qualify the students at the university to live in their favorite dormitory:

(9) 01 A: So they interview I think and they like ask you why you
    02   want to be in the house and, but it's- I know for I House,
    03   it's pretty intense. For J House, it wasn't that big deal
    04   because, you know, it's Japanese people- there are not that
    05   many people who want to speak Japanese all the time so-
    06 B: [hhhhhhhhh]
    07 C: [hhh   ]
    08 A: *I mean* there are a few of us, you know.
    09 C: A couple of million, yeah.   (CRMTP 4)

In lines 01 through 05, the speaker A says that teachers in his university interview students who want to live in I House (International House) and J House (Japanese House) by asking why they want to live there. How well they perform in the interview determines whether they are assigned to the former (which is popular and very competitive), while the interview matters less for the latter. This is because according to A, few people want to speak Japanese all the time, and his statement made the other interlocutors laugh. Considering there was a Japanese organizer recording their talk in the same room, it can be said that the addition of the proviso, *I mean* in line 08 is a consequence of A's consideration for the organizer who came all the way from Japan only to collect speech data. On the other hand, in the next example, the motivation for using *I mean* is not based on the speaker's consideration for others but on his anticipation of what the hearer will think:

(10) 01 A: My residents had problems with leaving their things out in
     02   the common room last year. They would always like leave out
     03   their laptops, and some of them didn't have passwords and
     04   then they would like go into a room and play Super Smash
     05   Brothers. And so if I saw that, I would- ***I mean***, I probably
     06   wasn't supposed to, but I would just like open their laptop
     07   like if they had Facebook open, I'd be like,
     08 B: Facebook break ...
     09 A: Like all these things that are Justin Bieber, like, like all of
     10   these of Rebecca Black.   (CRMTP 2)

In (10), speaker A mentions her experience of living in a dormitory. She did not like her roommates to leave their laptops out in the common room. She says she felt tempted to access their Facebook accounts. By *I mean*, the speaker here is not correcting, adding information, showing intention or consideration, or taking a turn, but showing that she knows using another's computer without permission is inappropriate. More importantly, the speaker also knows that the interlocutor thinks the same way. At the end of line 04 and 05, the speaker anticipates how the hearer thinks about her act and uses *I mean* to make it explicit. The primary feature of this usage is that the speaker uses a glottal stop to interrupt their own ongoing utterance; the reference is not to propositional content but the anticipated reaction of the interlocutor.

As shown in examples (4) through (10), there are various uses of *I mean* in which a speaker refers to propositional content, intention, turn, face, and anticipated reaction. In this study, a cognitive linguistic account is used to explain why speakers use *I mean* and how its various usages relate to each other: The speaker uses it for intersubjective adjustments, which are realized at various levels of discourse.

2.3 Dominant Occurrences

Depending on the standard of classification, the statistical analysis of data shows varying results. In Tanaka and Ishizaki (1994), the frequency of the different usages of *I mean* according to functions and positions in discourse is shown in Table 2.1.

	Initial	Medial	Final	Total
Addition of Relevant Information	18	0	0	18
Repair	3	10	0	13
Emphasize	0	0	5	5
Reason	14	0	0	14
Clarification	17	0	0	17
Stammer	4	2	0	6
Disagreement	6	0	0	6
Cutting-in	7	0	0	7
Conclusion	3	1	0	4
Total	72	13	5	90

Table 2.1: Functions and positions of *I mean*   (Tanaka and Ishizaki 1994: 15)[2]

Data in Tanaka and Ishizaki (1994: 12) consist of 30,000 words in three- to four-minute conversations on 25 different topics. As indicated in Table 2.1, *I mean* is frequently used to add information to or clarify what was mentioned in his prior discourse. On the other hand, Muzikant (2007) reported that 88 per cent of all tokens in face-to-face conversations function as monitoring or mistake-editing, while there are no tokens, which function as emphasizers or verbal fillers. While each study raises different pragmatic functions of frequently occurring functions, most of them agree that *I mean* occurs overwhelmingly in the initial or medial position of a sentence, clause or turn, but rarely at the end (e.g., Erman 1987: 50; Tanaka and Ishizaki 1994: 15; Brinton 2008; 118–119). Although various numbers are presented in this book, the aim of this study is to provide a theoretical explanation for why speakers use *I mean*. It will be proven that the use of *I mean* is for "intersubjective adjustment" as it has its fundamental basis in basic human cognitive abilities with ample evidence in both actually used and artificial realizations.

Here, I introduce Kobayashi (2013), a report of my fieldwork on discourse markers undertaken in the United States in 2012. Through the program entitled the Kanazawa University Cultural Resource Manager Training Program (CRMTP), I visited Tufts University, a private university located in the suburbs of Boston, Massachusetts. Tufts students come not only from all over the United States, but from around the world. During fieldwork, I asked the informants to engage in relaxed conversation on random topics for 15 to 30 minutes. The topics varied, although most related to the university, such as classes, teachers, life in dormitory, the city of Boston, dating, politics, sexism, and racism. The collected data amounted to approximately seven and a half hours of conversation and consisted of 19 conversation groups each containing two to four people. As shown in Tables 2.2 and 2.3, almost all of the informants were undergraduates, and 87% of all the informants could be considered native speakers of English, though the rest of them have high fluency in English.

Age	18	19	20	21	22	24	Total
Number	17	12	12	10	2	1	54

Table 2.2: Age of informants

Informants and their parents are both native English speakers	27 (50%)
Informants are native and their parents are non-native	20 (37%)
Both informants and their parents are non-native	7 (13%)

Table 2.3: Language background of informants

Table 2.4 shows a list of the discourse markers the informants used and their frequency.

Discourse Markers	Total
like	2203
I mean	225
you know	210
so	131
but	87
well	85
actually	46
I guess	30
I think	27
though	22
because	17
and	10
apparently	6
oh	4
or	4
then	2

Table 2.4: Token frequency of discourse markers in CRMTP data

In Table 2.4, the frequency of *like* is remarkably high; informants used *like* once every 12.4 seconds, on average. Jucker and Smith (1998: 176) reported a similar tendency; *like* is used once every 17 seconds on average in their data, collected at CSULB (California State University, Long Beach). They asked the participants to join two 15 minute-long sessions one week apart, and they had nine new participants join only in the latter session so that they could investigate if the difference between the strangers and friends affected the use of discourse markers. As shown in Table 2.5, they indicated the difference actually affects the frequency of *like*; the frequency in the former case is 1.6 times higher than that in the latter.

	Strangers	Friends	Total
like	2.8	4.5	3.5
you know	1.0	1.4	1.2
well	0.6	1.3	0.9
I mean	0.6	0.5	0.5
Total	5.0	7.6	6.1

Table 2.5: Frequency of markers (average number of tokens per minute) in conversations between pairs of strangers and pairs of friends
(Ibid. 178)

Interestingly, while an obvious increase in frequency can be seen for an adverb *like* and interjection *well*, not so much of a difference emerged for lexical phrases *you know* and *I mean*.

The reason why data from CRMTP has many instances of *like* may be because most of the informants were taking or had taken the same classes and hence knew each other (since I asked for volunteers for my research from language/linguistic-related classes) or because I did not specify topics and requested a casual atmosphere.

In Table 2.6 shows the usage and frequency of *I mean* based on data in CRMTP. The propositional content level seems to be the most frequently used for usages of *I mean*, followed by the turn level and implicature/speech-act level.

Usages of *I mean*		Total		Proportion	
Propositional Content Level		91		40.4%	
Implicature/Speech-act Level		47		20.9%	
Face Level		4		1.8%	
Turn Level	Turn-keeping	71	44	31.6%	19.6%
	Turn-taking		27		12.0%
Others		12		5.3%	
Total		225		100%	

Table 2.6: Type frequency of *I mean* in CRMTP data

Notes

1 In this study, the term "proposition" or something being "propositional" does not necessarily mean a sentence with truth-conditional content, but it is defined more broadly and schematically as a process expressed by a finite clause, including occurrence (that non-finite clause expresses) and epistemic status, following Langacker's definition (Langacker 1991: 498, 2008: 441).
2 The labels of the usages of *I mean* were originally in Japanese, and translated into English by the author. Unless otherwise noted, the author takes full responsibility for the English translation of what was originally in Japanese.

CHAPTER 3

Background

3.1 Introduction

There may be little objection to the idea that "speakers use discourse markers to help hearers understand what speakers mean in their prior and/or following discourse." The elements of text, speaker and hearer as well as how they are related to each other are the main concern in the discussions on the use of discourse markers. Previous studies can be organized as follows:

>   Approach 1. Text Analysis (e.g., Halliday and Hassan 1976)
>   Approach 2. Discourse Analysis (e.g., Schourup 1985; Schiffrin 1987)
>   Approach 3. Corpus Linguistics (e.g., Biber et al. 1999)
>   Approach 4. Pragmatics (e.g., Levinson 1983)
>   (Hirose and Matsuo 2015: 323–326)

In this study, approaches 2 and 4 are adopted; through detailed and careful analysis of examples and their contexts, the motivation of using the specific discourse marker and the organic relation of its usages are described in terms of pragmatic and cognitive linguistic theories. As repeatedly mentioned in this book, the hearer is our main concern and we believe it drives the speaker to use *I mean*.

The discourse marker *I mean* has been analyzed not only from a pragmatic perspective but from those of other areas as well, such as syntax, phonology, semantics, and historical linguistics. Although *the discourse-pragmatic functions of 'I mean' in Present-day English have been extensively studied* (Brinton 2008: 112), the characteristics noted in these studies merely show how and when *I mean* is used in conversation, but not why it is used by speakers. Moreover, in classifications, the relationships among categories have not been clarified. The nature of the use of the expression must be theoretically grounded and based on a theory that accommodates various types of linguistic phenomena. The present study aims at present an account for why a speaker uses *I mean*, and how the usages of *I mean* relate to each other from pragmatic and cognitive linguistic perspectives. More precisely, cognitive linguistic perspectives must incorporate pragmatic ones. Before embarking on any theoretical discussions, it is necessary to summarize a review previous studies. The purpose of this chapter is to provide background information on the study of *I mean*: its diachronic development, major previous studies, and their critical problems.

3.2 Chronological Change

The theory that semantic change shows a certain direction of change is called "unidirectionality" (cf. Hopper and Traugott 1993; Traugott and Dasher 2002). Traugott and Dasher (2002) show some patterns in diachronic semantic change, as in Figure 3.1.

truth-conditional	>			non-truth-conditional
content	>	content/procedural	>	procedural
s-w-proposition	>	s-o-proposition	>	s-o-discourse
nonsubjective	>	subjective	>	intersubjective

Figure 3.1: Correlated paths of directionality in semantic change (s-w = scope within; s-o = scope over) (Ibid. 40)

In diachronic semantic change in general, truth-conditional meaning tends to be changed into non-truth-conditional meaning, content meaning tends to shift to procedural meaning, linguistic elements referring to the content of proposition later acquire discourse functions, and non-subjective meanings tend to become intersubjective meanings. Specifically, the semantic change of discourse markers becomes such that linguistic elements with conceptual content change into those with pragmatic functions such as discourse connections, turn management, and attention-getters.

> DMs (discourse markers) ... typically arise out of conceptual meanings and uses constrained to the argument structure of the clause. Over time, they not only acquire pragmatic meanings ... but also come to have scope over propositions. If they link discourses on a hierarchically similar level, i.e. if they function at the local level, they can be called "connectives." They may also come to have global functions, making larger structures, for example episode units in narrative (e.g. *then*), or, in conversation, conversational turns (e.g. *so*). (ibid. 156)

Syntactically, there seem to be two paths discourse markers have undergone, as shown in Figure 3.2.

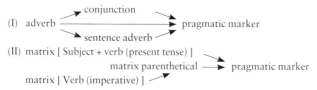

Figure 3.2: Syntactic development of pragmatic markers
(Brinton 2008: 246–251 quoted from Akimoto 2010: 9)

Two syntactic paths (I) and (II) start from the adverb, matrix clause with present tense verb, or the matrix verb in imperatives. The comment clause *I think* is an example of the development from a matrix to a pragmatic marker (i.e., Figure 3.2 (II)) (Akimoto 2010: 10).

As seen in Figures 3.1 and 3.2, there is a tendency toward unidirectionality in semantic change called "unidirectionality" (i.e., propositional → subjective → intersubjective) and also in the syntactic development of discourse markers (i.e., adverb/matrix → discourse markers).[1] It seems quite reasonable to conclude that *I mean* followed the same diachronic path with respect to its meaning and sentential position as other discourse markers and comment clauses. This is first because *I mean* is typical of expressions labeled discourse markers, and also because *I mean* is categorized as a comment clause (cf. Stenström 1995), since it consists of a first-person pronoun and a present tense verb. Moreover, *I mean* still maintains its usage as a matrix clause (e.g., *By X, Y mean Z.*) as well as a parenthetical. According to Brinton (2008), however, both semantic and syntactic change in *I mean* differ from those of other discourse markers and comment clauses. She says it is not the case that intersubjective meaning follows subjective meaning.

> ... there do seem to be some unidirectional patterns: for example, metalinguistic meanings tend to precede both metacommunicative/subjective and intersubjective meaning. However, in the case of *I mean* one cannot show that subjective meanings clearly precede intersubjective meanings.
>
> (ibid. 129)

	OE/ME	ME	EModE	PDE
metalinguistic/ metacommunicative	'I intend the previous discourse to signify/ have the meaning'	'I'm making the previous discourse more precise/ explicit' 'I'm reformulating the previous discourse (perhaps contrastively)'	'I'm repairing/ correcting the previous discourse'	'I'm exemplifying the previous discourse'
subjective				'I'm emphasizing the importance/ veracity of the previous discourse' 'I'm evaluating the previous discourse' 'I'm serious when I say'
intersubjective		'I'm implying more than I'm saying'		'I'm saying this because'

Table 3.1: The semantic development of *I mean* (Ibid. 128)

Table 3.1 indicates that an intersubjective use, such as *If that ye winsten what I mene* ("If you know what I mean") is seen for *I mean* in Middle English, whereas a subjective meaning such as *I mean it* is not seen until present-day English (PDE). Unlike the comment clause *I think*, whose fundamental role is to represent the speaker's epistemic status, *I mean* can be said to be intersubjective in nature in that replacement of propositional information and the clarification of the speaker's intention by using *I mean* are for the benefit of the hearer.

> ... the metalinguistic meanings 'I'm making this previous discourse more precise' and 'I'm exemplifying the previous discourse' also have an intersubjective quality, with the speaker attending to the hearer's need for more explicitness or for exemplification. (ibid. 129)

I mean is generally not used in monologues. I claim that it is used only when a speaker realizes that a certain piece of unintended information or implicature would be conveyed to the hearer, or when he realizes other discourse meanings or habits would affect the hearer.

Syntactically, the discourse marker *I mean* derives neither from the matrix clause nor from a sentential adverb. In the major corpora of Old English and Middle English, according to Brinton (2008: 124), *I mean* with a *that* complement accounts for 8% of uses, and the form *as/so/which I mean* together with a phase accounts for 69%. Based on these data, she suggested that the source of the development of *I mean* as a discourse marker (a parenthetical in her terms) was *I mean* followed by a phrase:

> ... it seems clear that the origin of parenthetical *I mean* cannot be found in either of these structures (matrix clause + nominal *that*-clause or

sentential relative). The predominant structure – *I mean* followed by a phrasal category – is the most likely source of this parenthetical structure. (ibid. 127)

She continues to describe the process of its development as follows:

I mean governs a phrasal element ({NP, VP, AP, PP, AdP})[2] and has scope within the sentence. The bonds between *I mean* and the phrasal element are weakened or loosened, and *I mean* can begin to be postposed to the phrasal element. ... *I mean* as a syntactically free parenthetical with scope over the sentence. (ibid. 127)

Here, at the end of this section, I aim to mention the relation between politeness and semantic change. Finell (1992) indicates that politeness can be one of the causes of semantic changes of pragmatic markers. Akimoto (2002: 206–207) follows the change of the verb *pray* and finds that its subjective meaning has strengthened; therefore, propositional meaning was lost and only the politeness function was left. After the 19th century, this usage of *pray* disappeared and was replaced by *please*. Traugott and Dasher (2002) seem to consider the semantic change of politeness a process of intersubjectification.

Intersubjective meanings crucially involve social deixis (attitude toward status that speakers impose on first person – second person deixis). They impact directly on the self-image or "face" needs of SP/W or AD/R.[3]
(ibid. 23)

Although I have not investigated whether *I mean* has acquired a meaning of politeness, it seems probable that politeness enhances the use of *I mean*, but is not entailed in its meaning. As indicated by Fox Tree and Schrock (2002: 733–734), when a less face-threatening action follows *I mean*, the speaker redresses the threat not with *I mean* itself, but in the following utterance. They claim that the relation between the face-threatening and face-saving is still maintained even after omitting *I mean*. Moreover, saving face is the least frequently occurring function of *I mean*, as shown in Table 2.6. For the reasons above, in this study, the usage of politeness (i.e., the use of *I mean* to save the hearer's face) is established in synchronic (not in diachronic) analysis of *I mean*, and face-saving should be considered one of the speaker's motivations for using *I mean*. From a chronological standpoint, this usage is not thoroughly established as a part of its meaning.

3.3 Previous Studies and Their Empirical Problems

3.3.1 Schiffrin (1987)

Schiffrin (1987: 31) defined discourse markers *as sequentially dependent elements which bracket units of talk,* and showed that they function to maintain local coherence in some levels of discourse ("planes of talk" in her terms), introducing a model of discourse (Figure 3.3).

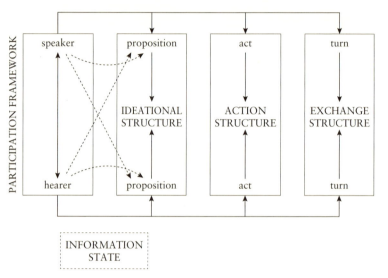

Figure 3.3: A discourse model (Ibid. 25)

The large square located on the right represents a structure of turn exchange called the exchange structure. This structure also includes the notion of an adjacency pair such as question/answer, offer/accept, and greeting/greeting. The structure to the left of the exchange structure is called the action structure, which includes intended and actual preceding, current, and subsequent actions. While the exchange structure is based on conversational rules or repetitive habits practiced by everyone participating in the conversation, the action structure is based on expected linguistic and cultural customs whose absence offends the hearer or makes him uncomfortable. The ideational structure, located to the left of the action structure, represents the relation or exchange of propositions, which is the basis for cohesive relations, topic relations, and functional relations. The difference between the first two structures and the third is described as follows:

In contrast to exchange and action structures (which I view as pragmatic because of the central role which speakers and hearers play in negotiating their organization), the units within this (ideational) structure are semantic: they are propositions, or what I'll just call ideas. (ibid. 25–26)

... idea structures differ from action and exchange structures because they consist of linguistic units (propositions with semantic content), whereas exchange and action structures emerge through units (turns and acts) which are realized by the use of language, but are not linguistic *per se*. (ibid. 26)

The participation framework located on the extreme left represents the organization of participants in the conversation. Teacher-student and doctor-patient relations are cases of unequally balanced participation frameworks. The dotted arrows connecting elements in different structures illustrate the dynamic exchange actions between the speaker and hearer. For example, when a dispute shifts into a fight, the interlocutors initially exchange propositions, each one referring to the other's propositional content, but then, as it proceeds to a fight, the burden of the conversation shifts to certain speech acts such as criticizing and insulting and to holding and taking turn of the conversation (i.e., each speaker attempts to hold their turn as long as possible and to take it back again as soon as possible). In other words, the dotted arrows show what the speaker or hearer is responsible for in each element of conversation.[4] The information state located at the bottom of the figure indicates meta-information, such as the speaker's self-knowledge (i.e., information on what the speaker knows about what he knows) and speaker's knowledge about the hearer (i.e., information on what the speaker knows about what the hearer knows). Such information continues to be updated following the flow of discourse.

Based on careful observations on speech data, Schiffrin (1987) shows the relation between the use of discourse markers and the speaker's and hearer's knowledge, propositional contents, speech acts, and turn exchanges (Figure 3.4).

Information State	Participation Framework	Ideational Structure	Action Structure	Exchange Structure
*oh	oh		oh	
well	*well	well	well	well
		*and	and	and
		*but	but	but
		*or		or
so	so	*so	so	so
because		*because	because	
	now	*now		
then		*then	then	
I mean	*I mean	I mean		
*y'know	y'know	y'know		y'know

Figure 3.4: Planes of talk on which markers function (Ibid. 316)

Asterisks in Figure 3.4 represent a primary function of each discourse marker. *I mean* is defined as a marker *marking a speaker's upcoming modification of the meaning of his/her prior talk* (ibid. 296). As depicted in the figure above, it functions primarily in a participation framework as the modification is originated by the speaker. It functions secondarily in an information state and ideational structure because *I mean* is used to signal the speaker's commitment to the proposition in his previous utterance and also to attract the hearer's attention to the preceding utterance.[5]

The modifications of speaker ideas and intentions, *I mean*'s two major meanings, derive from the two original meanings of the verb *mean* (ibid. 296). The two original meanings correspond to what are known as in expressions: *X mean Y* and *X don't mean to Y* (Leech 1983). *I mean* in the following examples reflects these two meanings.

(11) a. But I think um ten years from now,
 b. it's going to be much more liberal.
 c. I could see it in my own job.
 d. ***I mean**, when I started working for the government, there were no colored people.
 e. And today eh ... uh ... twenty five, thirty percent, forty percent of the people I work with are- are colored. (Schiffrin 1987: 296)

(12) a. He says, "Oh, I wish you could come with me!"
 b. And I said—I was very pro- proper and prim!
 c. And I said, "Oh, I couldn't go away with you."
 d. And he says, "*I mean* let's get married!"
 e. And I said, "Oh, okay!" (= (3))

In (11), before *I mean*, the speaker mentions a liberalizing atmosphere in his company, and after *I mean*, he brings up an actual event to support his statement. In other words, his idea (i.e., *I could see it in my job.*) is expanded in the utterance following *I mean* (d–e). In (12), on the other hand, the speaker does not explain or provide an example of the propositional content but explicitly shows his intention after *I mean*. Note that the modification with *I mean* in the latter example is driven by the speaker's doubt about whether the hearer understands the speaker's intention.

> *Meaning* and *I mean* both preface explanations of intention, particularly when the intended force of an action is deemed to have been missed by a recipient, e.g. because it was too indirect for appropriate uptake.
> (Schiffrin 1987: 296)[6]

Unlike the discourse marker *you know*, *I mean* does not work in an exchange structure. This is because *I mean*'s primary function, the speaker's orientation to modifications, is not compatible with taking a turn from the hearer. In fact, as shown in the following example, *I mean* has only limited power to take a turn from another interlocutor.

(13) Freda: a. Now if you're drowning, you're gonna fight t'
           ⎡t'save s-   ⎤
      Jack: b. ⎣You're not⎦ gonna say "Well this is it! I'm gonna let go!"
               c. It doesn't work that way.
      Debby: d. Yeh that makes sense.
      Jack: e. ⎡Your cockroach ... you wanna⎤ step on a cockroach, =
      Freda: f. ⎣*I mean* e- even if- even if-⎦
      Jack: g. = what does it do?   ⎡When you're⎤ ready- =
      Freda: h.   I think even ⎣a person-   ⎦
      Jack: i. = it'll run! Wouldn't it?   (Ibid. 308)

In (13f), Freda starts her utterance with *I mean*, thus, attempting to have a turn in the conversation. However, *I mean* in line (f) is not strong enough to make Jack give up his turn.

Schiffrin (1987) emphasized that *I mean*'s functions are all centered on the speaker in that *I mean* marks a modification of the speaker's own idea and his own intention. *I mean* is not used to provide information to aid the hearer's understanding:

> This meaning (a speaker's upcoming modification of the ideas or intentions of a prior utterance) allows us to understand why *I mean* prefaces

repairs which display shifts in speakers' intentions, but not repairs which provide background information designed to supplement hearers' understanding of prior discourse. (ibid. 302–303)

However, this does not necessarily mean that *I mean* lacks hearer-related functions:

> ... *I mean* also maintains hearer focus on prior material: *I mean* instructs the hearer to continue attending to the material of prior text in order to hear how it will be modified. (ibid. 309)

I mean allows the hearer to focus on the speaker's previous utterance, which is a function of a so-called "attention-getter."

Schiffrin (1987) defines *I mean* as a marker for upcoming modification of a speaker's ideas and intentions; thus, it is intrinsically characterized by speaker orientation. In (13f), Freda starts her utterance with *I mean*, thus, attempting to have a turn in the conversation. However, *I mean* in line (f) is not strong enough to make Jack give up his turn. In the following example, neither of the idea nor the intention are modified.

(14) Our son had wandered home from college and brought the puppy with him. He - ***I mean*** Ariel - was pasty-faced and underachieving and piping up about responsibility and carbon footprints. (COCA)[7]

The speaker in (14) replaces *He* with *Ariel*, both of which indicate the same individual. Although the speaker initiated this modification, it was not done for the sake of the speaker, but the hearer. The example above shows that *I mean* is used not only to help the hearer focus but also to aid his understanding of the propositional content of the previous utterance. Therefore, the hearer's understating should be a major consideration in the speaker's modification of his idea. It is evident from example (14) that the hearer (or hearer's understanding) motivates the speaker to use *I mean*.

3.3.2 Fox Tree and Schrock (2002)

The aims of Fox Tree and Schrock (2002) were similar to those of this book: to clarify the purpose of the use of *I mean* (and *you know*) and its basic meanings in terms of the purposes of its use, which had not been agreed upon by researchers. They quoted Schiffrin (1987: 304) and defined the basic meaning of *I mean* as *to indicate upcoming adjustments, from the word level to the negotiation of meaning* (ibid. 741). More specifically, adjustments by *I mean* are classified into five categories: interpersonal, turn management, repair, monitoring, and organization. In its interpersonal use, *I mean* is used to spontaneously adjust ongoing speech (for example, to save the hearer's face). The second use relates to turn management, and the third includes repairs of various levels, from syntactic and phonological repairs to mental repairs (e.g., changing one's mind). In monitoring, the speaker modifies the hearer's understanding using *I mean*, and organization relates to more global adjustments such as topic shifts.

What makes the analysis of Fox Tree and Schrock (2002) remarkable is their focus on the purpose of using *I mean* and on the relationship between the speaker and hearer (e.g., interpersonal, turn management, and monitoring), rather than between the speaker and what is said. In showing the relation between the use of *I mean* and face-saving, they argue that face-saving is not a function directly associated with *I mean*, since without *I mean*, face is threatened in the previous utterance and saved in the following utterance (see example (9)) (ibid. 733–734). They develop this argument by asserting that uttering *I mean* by itself serves to save face:

> *I mean* may be linked with positive politeness because using it reminds conversational participants of more casual talk. At the same time, it may be linked to negative politeness by decreasing face threat; saying *I mean* may be like saying "I'm not committed to what I just said and will adjust if you are offended."　　　　　　　　　　　　　　(ibid. 741–742)

As noted above, *I mean* relates to positive politeness, or consideration of hearer's desire for friendliness, as the use of *I mean* reflects casual conversation, and it also relates to negative politeness, or consideration of hearer's desire for not being interfered, since the use of *I mean* weakens the speaker's commitment to what has been said.

Their central questions of why *I mean* is used and how the hearer relate to the motivation for its use are tremendously important. However, they do not further discuss on how the basic meanings relate to each other and what the levels upon which adjustments by *I mean* are based. Taking careful stock of university students' conversations, as will be discussed in detail later, this study also revealed that the speaker does save the hearer's face, keep turns, and watch the hearer's understanding when using *I mean*. The cognitive linguistic perspective, I believe, can lead to a rational theoretical account of these phenomena.

3.3.3 Imo (2005)

Using a Construction Grammar approach, Imo (2005) analyzed the syntactic, prosodic, semantic, and pragmatic characteristics of *I mean*. Imo (2005) divides the synchronic functions of *I mean* into two categories: textual function and interpersonal function. The former includes functions to lead repair, show concessions/concessive repair, conclusions, explications, parenthetical asides, and quoting. The latter includes change of perspective and marking of "disfluenz."[8] An example of change of perspective is shown below. The speaker takes a perspective toward others before *I mean* (lines 03–04), and then takes her own perspective after *I mean* (lines 05–07):

(15) 01 A:nd uh::m (.) I don't know i think that I'M in the Navy::.
      02 and there is a CHANCE that i could be called over THERE. .h
      03 a:nd i'm having a HARD time finding PEOple who can BURN
      04 FLAGS; calling themselves aMErican. (.)
      05 *i mean* (.) for ME:;
      06 i i could never do that as a civilian, (.)
      07 A:nd as being a NAvy person. (.)   (Imo 2005: 24)

In (15), the speaker, who is in the Navy, criticizes pacifists who burn American flags to protest against the United States' role in the Iraq War (lines 03–04). *I mean* in (15) indicates a perspective shift from pacifists who burns the flag of their own country back to the speaker herself.

Just as with idiomatic expressions, Imo (2005) considers *I mean* to consist of multiple constructions.[9] Table 3.2 shows the syntactic, prosodic, semantic, and pragmatic characteristics of the "*I mean* construction."

I mean	
Type of construction: complex, specific, free	
Syntax:	autonomous phrase, can be combined with other discourse markers
Topology:	tendency to be placed in an utterance-initial position
Prosody:	variable prosodic realization (own intonation contour, integrated into the intonation contour of the utterance it precedes, integrated into the intonation contour of some previous utterance)
Semantics:	bleached semantics; only in some cases residual traces of the original semantic content of *to mean* are activated
Pragmatics:	projective power: some further utterance is expected after *I mean*
Function:	general indexical function: cut-marker
	specific functions are context-dependent and are mainly textual ones; interpersonal functions are only secondary

Table 3.2: The constructional schema of the *I mean* construction   (Ibid. 30)

The *I mean* construction has two pragmatic functions: textual and interpersonal. As shown in the lower part of Table 3.2, the former is the primary and the latter the secondary function. Although these two functions can be segmented further into other discourse functions depending on contexts, that is Imo's (2005) concern: The shared commonalities are the functions of pragmatic projection and the cut marker:

> The two central and common functional features that all uses of *I mean* seem to have, are the following:
> - *I mean* always opens a pragmatic projection, signalling to the recipients that there is something to follow.
> - It acts as a "cut-marker," semantically and/or syntactically interrupting the ongoing flow of utterances and framing the utterance following *I mean* as not to be interpreted as a seamless continuation of the utterance preceding *I mean*. (ibid. 15)

In other words, *I mean* acts as a semantic and/or syntactic boundary of discourse and also signals some subsequent utterance. The *I mean* construction constitutes a construction network just like that of other constructions.[10] Table 3.3 illustrates that the *I mean* construction inherits its characteristics from the more schematic discourse markers construction and complement-taking verb *to mean* construction.

Discourse Markers
Type of construction: complex/atomistic, schematic, free
Syntax: autonomous phrase; can be combined with other discourse markers
Topology: tendency to be placed in utterance-initial position
Prosody: variable prosodic realization
Semantics: bleached semantics
Function: general indexical function; textual or interpersonal functions depending on type of discourse marker and context

Complement-taking verb *to mean*
Type of construction: complex, specific/ schematic, free
Syntax: verb with a syntactic projection in terms of valence; complement can take a variety of forms (clause with or without complementizer, noun phrase, adjective phrase etc.)
Topology: initial position
Prosody: usually one intonation contour
Semantics: full semantics: *to refer to*
Function: making clear what one has been talking about/what one had in one's mind when talking about something; correcting other person's misunderstandings of what one has been saying/thinking

---

Table 3.3: The constructional schemas of the discourse marker construction and the complement-taking verb *to mean* construction (Ibid. 31)

A comparison of Tables 3.2 and 3.3 shows that most of the characteristics of the *I mean* construction derive from the discourse markers construction except for the semantic characteristics and pragmatic functions, which derive from the complement-taking verb *to mean* construction. *I mean*'s pragmatic projection power originates from the syntactic projection of the latter construction.

By employing the Construction Grammar approach, Imo (2005) provided a network of *I mean* constructions and demonstrated how their characteristics relate to each other; this is portrayed in Figure 3.5.

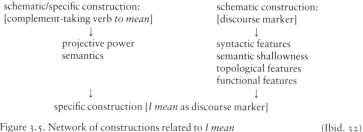

Figure 3.5. Network of constructions related to *I mean* (Ibid. 32)

Not only schematic but also specific characteristics of various research fields such as syntax and prosody are well organized. Nevertheless, Imo's (2005) main claims can be paraphrased as "*I mean* shares fundamental characteristics with other discourse markers and complement-taking verbs," which appears to be very reasonable in light of the description of discourse markers in Schiffrin (1987) and the semantic development discussed in Brinton (2008). However, the similarities between and connections among neighboring constructions are mentioned mainly so that the richness of specific functions of *I mean* are not viewed. This study also lacks a theoretical account for how the specific functions of *I mean* relate to each other and what motivates speakers to use it.

3.3.4 Brinton (2008)

Brinton (2008) mainly focuses on the semantic and syntactic change in "comment clauses" (cf. Quirk et al. 1985: 1112–1118) including *say, look, see, I mean, If you will,* and *as it were,* but also offers a synchronic classification and theoretical account that posits nine pragmatic meanings of *I mean* (including subcategories) derived from its original meanings.

> …, in addition to the "full" meaning of 'intention,' I identify five pragmatic meanings of *I mean*: (a) appositional meanings (repair, reformulation, explicitness, and exemplification), (b) causal meaning, (c) expressions of speaker attitude (evaluation and sincerity), and (e) inter-

personal meaning. (ibid. 114)[11]

Although Brinton's (2008) classification is based on the verb *mean*'s two original meanings (cf. Leech 1983; Schiffrin 1987), those two meanings are hardly used as parentheticals in PDE; instead, they are seen in the forms with a *to* infinitive or complement phrase/clause such as in *I mean to V, what I mean is, by X I mean* (Brinton 2008: 114). The first type of pragmatic meaning is appositional meanings, and includes four subcategories: repair, reformulation, explicitness, and exemplification. These meanings are metalinguistic/ metacommunicative in the sense that they refer to what is coded in the previous utterance and how the previous utterance is expressed (ibid. 114). *I mean* of causal meaning can be paraphrased by *because* or *I'm saying this because* and is both subjective and intersubjective:

> As the speaker is being attentive to the hearer's need for explanation, this usage is intersubjective. It is also subjective since the utterance preceding *I mean* usually expresses a personal opinion or view of the speaker. (ibid. 116)

The other two pragmatic meanings are labeled expressions of speaker attitude and interpersonal meaning; the former *I mean* is subjective in that it expresses emphasis, evaluation, and sincerity from/of the speaker, while the latter, which includes phrases such as *if you understand what I mean* and *you see what I mean*, is intersubjective in that the second-person pronoun *you* is coded, that is, the intersubjective attitude is semanticized into the expression.

For the derivation of various pragmatic meanings, her argument goes as follows:

> By the Gricean Maxim of Manner "be brief [avoid unnecessary prolixity]" (1975: 46) or Levinson's "M-Heuristic" "what's said in an abnormal way isn't normal" (2000), hearers will make the inference that the same information is not simply being restated but that some additional information is being presented. (Brinton 2008: 129)[12]

In other words, by repeating similar information before and after *I mean*, when *I mean* and the utterance that follows interrupts the discourse, the speaker prompts the hearer to infer the special meaning of invited inference. The process of how the invited inference is generated is shown below.

> (a) the information in the previous utterance is being corrected
> *I'll see you tomorrow morning, I mean, afternoon.*

+> 'afternoon is the correct time'
(b) the information in the previous utterance is being more precisely or more explicitly expressed
The situation could be embarrassing, I mean, politically.
+> 'the situation is not generally embarrassing, but the precise way in which it could be embarrassing is in a political way' (ibid. 129)[13]

Although Brinton's (2008) specific classification helps us understand how *I mean* is used, the chronological explanation for the process of inference is too vague to apply to the synchronic account of all the meanings. First, it does not explain why the repetition of similar information causes particular meanings such as repair and causal meaning, but not other meanings such as agreement or counterfactuality, for example. Second, the relation between each pragmatic meaning is unclear. Third, an account based on invited inferences cannot distinguish *I mean* for correction of propositional content (= (16)) from *I mean* for better hearer understanding (= (17)), as it disregards the purpose for which the speaker uses it.

(16) I haven't been to Florida. *I mean*, I have. (= (1))
(17) He - *I mean* Ariel - (Excerpt from (14))

3.3.5 Other Previous Studies

The studies previously mentioned classify the pragmatic functions of *I mean* from discourse analysis, Construction Grammar, and historical linguistics perspectives. It goes without saying that other perspectives such as syntactic position and prosody, must also be taken into consideration. This section provides a brief summary of such analysis.

Tanaka and Ishizaki (1994) analyze the relation between pragmatic functions and the syntactic positions of *I mean*; the token frequency of clause-initial *I mean* is quite high, while the clause final frequency is very low (as shown in Table 2.1), and the function of emphasizing the previous utterance is limited to the latter position.

Dehé and Wichmann (2010) discuss the relation between pragmatic functions and the prosodic characteristics of comment clauses. They argue that the differences in semantic/pragmatic meaning affect on prosodic realizations: Comment clauses referring to propositional content tend to form independent units, called an intonation units (IUs) and have a stress inside the domain. Clauses that benefit the hearer (e.g., the "interpersonal" function) have an IU integrated into a neighboring IU and thus have no stress. The pitch level of those functioning as fillers is maintained inside IU. Therefore, the shift from comment clauses with high reflection of their original meanings to functional ones suggest that prosodic characteristics are being lost. As mentioned above, Dehé and Wichmann (2010) insist that the functional and prosodic characteristics are correlated (though their investigations are mainly on *I think* and *I suppose*), while Imo (2005) cited similar prosodic realizations of *I mean*, but did not explicitly argue for their correlation.

3.4 Summary

In previous studies, the discourse markers *I mean* and *you know* have been compared in terms of their pragmatic functions; the relation between the speaker and propositional content is argued for more in the former while the one between the speaker and hearer or propositional content and the hearer is argued for more in the latter (e.g., Schiffrin 1987; Tanaka and Ishizaki 1994; Fox Tree and Schrock 2002). Recently, however, the focus of the study of *I mean* has shifted to the speaker–hearer relationship, with Fox Tree and Schrock (2002) proposing "interpersonal" interaction and "monitoring" as its basic meanings. In terms of chronological change, Brinton (2008) indicated that *I mean* followed a typical process of grammaticalization, except that there is no clear evidence that the subjective meaning preceded its intersubjective meaning. She showed two possible paths of syntactic development: *I mean* starting as a matrix clause first occurring only in clause-initial position, and, as grammaticalization proceeded, expanding to clause-internal and final positions (Imo 2005; Brinton 2008).

This chapter introduced and provided a critical analysis of major studies on *I mean*. Previous studies showed in full detail how *I mean* is used in various contexts but gave little attention to the speakers' motivation for using it or the relationships among its various usages. Schiffrin (1987) presented two major pragmatic meanings/functions, Tanaka and Ishizaki (1994) posited nine, Fox Tree and Schrock (2002) identified five basic meanings, Imo (2005) proposed two overarching categories and eight subcategories, and Brinton (2008) argued for nine divisions. None of these studies accounted for how these multiple categories can be ordered and correlated. Moreover, although some researchers dispute the historical linguistic, syntactic, and prosodic features of *I mean*, they prefer comparing the characteristics of *I mean* to those of discourse markers in general to tracking down the question of why specific characteristics are only observed in the particular function of *I mean*.

This study provides, in terms of pragmatic and cognitive linguistic theories, a theoretical background for why the speaker uses *I mean* and how the usages relate to each other. In short, the speaker uses *I mean* for intersubjective adjustment, and the variation in its usages can be attributed to different cognitive processes between the two conceptualizers, the speaker and hearer. Among the basic human cognitive concepts motivating the use of *I mean* are specificity, reference point relationships, and intersubjectivity.

Notes

1 According to Traugott and Dasher (2002: 24), *from a historical perspective, subjectification precedes intersubjectification*.
2 NP, VP, AP, PP, and AdP stand for noun phrase, verb phrase, adjective phrase, prepositional phrase, and adverb phrase, respectively.
3 SP/W and AD/R stand for speaker/writer and addressee/reader, respectively.
4 Schiffrin (1987) describes the notion of "participation framework" as follows:
    ... participation frameworks involve not only the different footings through which speaker and hearer relate to each other, but the ways in which producers of talk are related to the units of talk they are producing – their propositions, acts, and turns.
    (Schiffrin 1987: 295).
5 As shown in Figure 3.4, modification of propositional content is not *I mean*'s primary function. The markers that have primary structure in ideational structure are *and*, *but*, and *or*, which are derived from conjunctions. For markers to have their primary function in ideational structure means that they reflect their original meanings of components.
    ... those markers with meaning have their primary functions on ideational planes of talk, and those without meaning show the reverse tendency.   (Schiffrin 1987: 319)
6 Stenström (1994) and Fox Tree and Schrock (2002) refered to the relation between *I mean* and the hearer's understanding thereof.
    Sometimes the speaker needs to make a new start or rephrase what s/he was going to say in the middle of a turn, often because the listener shows that s/he cannot follow or is not convinced. In such situations the <monitor> *I mean* comes in handy: ...
    (Stenström (1994: 131))
    The forewarning adjustments function also sits well with speaker's increased monitoring of addressee comprehension after *I mean*. If speakers have just forewarned an adjustment, they might seek an acknowledgement of understanding from the addressee has been made. (Fox Tree and Schrock 2002: 742)
    Intersubjective adjustment, the motivation of using *I mean*, which has been discussed throughout this book, is based on this type of speaker's doubt; whether or not his message is conveyed to the hearer or the hearer's comprehension is monitored. In other words, one of central arguments of this book is that such doubt is the very motivation of using *I mean*, and that pragmatic and cognitive linguistic theories provide a rational account for it. In the following example, *I don't mean rich. I mean, rich*, the speaker is trying to adjust the hearer's expectation to be as extreme as that of the speaker.
    (18) Fifteen years ago, if somebody had come up to you in the projects and said, you know, you're going to be rich and I don't mean rich, *I mean*, rich,   (COCA)
7 Corpus of Contemporary American English (http://corpus.byu.edu/coca/)
8 Imo (2005: 26–27) quoted the term "Disfluenz" from Fischer (1992); it indicates techniques of "disfluent" talk, such as signaling a problem in the speaker's thoughts and saving face.
9 In Construction Grammar and Cognitive Linguistics, a "construction" is considered a

conventional unit composed of form and meaning, and constructions that share similar characteristics form a polysemy network (cf. Goldberg 2006).
10 See note 13 above.
11 The original text appears to misprint *four* as *five* (pragmatic meanings) and *(d)* as *(e)*.
12 See Levinson (2000) for the relation between M heuristic and Grice's Maxim of Manner.

> The third (M) heuristic ("what's said in an abnormal way isn't normal") can be related directly to Grice's maxim of Manner ("Be perspicuous"), specifically to his first submaxim "avoid obscurity of expression" and his fourth "avoid prolixity." (ibid. 38)

13 The following shows the other invited inferences of *I mean* listed in Brinton (2008).
   (c) a contrastive reformulation of the information in the previous utterance is being presented
   I just want to look at, I mean, examine the evidence.
   +> 'I do not want to have a (quick) look but rather a thorough examination of the evidence'
   (d) a particular example or instance of the information in the previous utterance is being supplied
   He really knows how to cook. I mean, he can even make soufflés.
   +> 'An example of his ability is his ability to make soufflés (his ability could manifest itself in other ways)'
   (e) the information in the previous utterance is emphasized or its accuracy is asserted by the speaker
   He's rich, I mean, (really) rich.
   +> 'I'm emphasizing the extent of his richness/I'm being emphatic about his richness'
   (ibid. 129)

CHAPTER 4

A Pragmatic Account of *I mean*

4.1 Introduction

This chapter offers a pragmatic account of the use of *I mean*. Previous studies have labeled the relationship between information before and after *I mean* and made it clear how *I mean* is used in conversations; however, it remains unclear what motivates speakers to use the expression. Here, I argue that using *I mean* signals either a violation of Grice's Conversational Maxims or an attempt to save face. The information referred to by *I mean* seems to comprise two types: In the first type, the speaker violates one of the maxims in the propositional content and implicature generated by the speaker in the previous utterance, which are respectively called the what-is-said level and the implicature level in this book.[1] Moreover, when the speaker uses *I mean* independently of the requirements of Grice's Maxims in the previous discourse, it also indicates face saving, in terms of Brown and Levinson's (1987) Politeness Theory: *I mean* marks a speaker's threat to the addressee's face in the previous utterance and the desire to disarm the threat in the following utterance. Though speakers have the choice of saying *I'm sorry, I mean* instead of simply saying *I mean*, English speakers rarely take this option. This can be explained as saving either the speaker's or the hearer's positive face. The speech act of apologizing causes a face threat to speaker's own PF; hence the speaker saves face by using only *I mean* without an expression of apology. In some cases, though, the speaker shows some sense of intimacy with the hearer by not apologizing; he or she shows that the misstatement before *I mean* is not worth apologizing for their relationship.

4.2 Analysis from Grice's Conversational Maxims

4.2.1 Grice's Cooperative Principle and the Four Maxims

In conversations, speakers do not have full responsibility for coding everything to convey their messages, but rather their utterance is usually designed to let hearers appreciate what they say and infer what the speaker intends to convey. Grice, in his famous 1989 work *Studies in the Way of Words*, terms the content of what the speaker actually uttered "what is said" and refers to the inference that the speaker intends to convey as the "implicature" (or "what is implicated"). As fundamental rules and tendencies of conversation, Grice presupposes the Cooperative Principle (CP) and four maxims: The maxims of Quantity, Quality, Relation, and Manner. Participants engage cooperatively in organized conversations in which the hearer tries to infer what the speaker intends to convey, even if the speaker's meaning does not correspond with what is literally said.[2] This can only be achieved if the speaker knows the hearer is cooperative and vice versa. Conversely, people would never make the effort to understand what is implicated, such as metaphors and irony, without presupposing the CP. The principle and the four maxims together describe how speakers provide implied meanings beyond coded meaning.

The CP and the four maxims are shown below.[3] Grice (1989: 26) describes the CP and the first maxim called Maxim of Quantity as follows:

> Make your conversational contribution such as is required, at the stage at which it occurs, by the accepted purpose or direction of the talk exchange in which you are engaged.
>
> 1. Make your contribution as informative as is required (for the current purpose of the exchange).
> 2. Do not make your contribution more informative than is required.

This maxim reflects the tendency of participants in a conversation to provide appropriate amounts of information. In the following example, the speaker flouts the maxim to produce a "particularized conversational implicature" (PCI).[4]

(19) A: Have you guys been to Australia before?
  B: He has.
(20) a. He has.
  b. +> I have never been to Australia[5]

Three participants (A, B, and C) are in conversation in (19), and speaker B implicates that he has not been to Australia by giving less information than required, by only mentioning C's visit (C corresponds to *He*). Grice also cites tautologies such as *Women are women* and *War is war* as examples of flouting the Maxim of Quantity (Grice 1989: 33).

The other maxims of Quality, Relation, and Manner are described as follows:

> Under the category of Quality falls a supermaxim – "Try to make your contribution one that is true" – and two more specific maxims:
> 1. Do not say what you believe to be false.
> 2. Do not say that for which you lack adequate evidence.
>
> Under the category of Relation I place a single maxim, namely, "Be relevant."
>
> Finally, under the category of Manner, which I understand as relating not (like the previous categories) to what is said but, rather, to *how* what is said is to be said, I include the supermaxim – "Be perspicuous" – and various maxims such as:
> 1. Avoid obscurity of expression.
> 2. Avoid ambiguity.
> 3. Be brief (avoid unnecessary prolixity).
> 4. Be orderly.

Metaphorical and ironic expressions are typical examples of deliberate flouting of the Maxim of Quality. By giving obviously false information, a speaker can imply something different or even opposite to the meaning of what is actually said. While the implicatures arising from these expressions are mostly context dependent, examples such as (21) can be generated in any context (called "generalized conversational implicatures" (GCIs)):

(21)   a. Kosuke and Mizue got married last summer.
         b. +> The speaker has concrete evidence for their marriage

When the speaker utters (21a), the hearer presupposes (21b), assuming (for example) that the speaker participated in the wedding ceremony or actually heard from the couple. Unlike (20), in which the speaker makes an implication by flouting a maxim, the speaker in (21a) implicates (21b) by adhering to the maxim.

Examples in which speakers clearly flout the Maxim of Relation are relatively scarce (Grice 1989: 35). Such a case would be, for example, if a participant suddenly interrupted a conversation with an utterance unrelated to the previous discourse. As an example, imagine three participants (let's call them A, B, and C) talking in A's house, B starts insulting C. In such a context, A's utterance *Guys, would you like to have some sweets?* obviously violates the Maxim of Relation, but would implicate speaker A's intention to request a change the topic or stop the quarrel. Even though A's utterance is completely irrelevant to the flow of the current conversation, the other participants could infer the speaker's meaning (e.g., *Stop it!*). In other words, even if a speaker does not follow the maxim on a surface level (the what-is-said level), the hearer anticipates that the speaker is adhering to the CP on a deeper level (the implicature level); thus, participants of the conversation attempt to seek what is implicated in the speaker's utterance.

The last of the four maxims, the Maxim of Manner, relates to the articulation of utterances: Be brief or avoid redundancy. The following is an example of the maxim being flouted:

(22)   Miss X produced a series of sounds that corresponded closely with the score of "Home Sweet Home."   (Grice 1989: 37)

Instead of saying simply *Miss X sang "Home Sweet Home,"* the speaker is intentionally verbose, implicating that her singing is terrible.

This section illustrates Grice's notions of "what is said" and "implicature" and how his CP and the four maxims contribute to the generation of implicatures. The following section argues that violations of Grice's four maxims are intimately related to speaker motivation for using *I mean*: Speakers use *I mean* to address the offense given in what is said or implicated in his previous discourse.

4.2.2 *I mean* at the What-Is-Said Level

Speakers sometimes use *I mean* because they think the literal meaning of a previous utterance was either incorrect or vague. In other words, *I mean* signals that the speaker violated the Grice's Maxim of Quality (or Manner) at what-is-said level in his previous utterance. It also signals the intention to obey the maxim in the utterance following *I mean*. In example (23) below, speakers J and N are both university students, and N asks in lines 02–03 if J has been to Florida before. J first responds that he has not been there, but then realizes that he actually has. Before *I mean*, J accidentally violates the Maxim of Quality since his utterance *I haven't been to Florida* is not what he believes to be true. But following *I mean*, he obeys the maxim by providing a truthful statement.

As in (23), *I mean* in (24) can also be considered a speaker's violation of the Maxim of Quality at what-is-said level.

(23) 01 J: Where in Florida are you from?
     02 N: I am from Melbourne, Florida. Have you been to Florida
     03   before?
     04 J: I haven't been to Florida. *I mean* I have. I've been to
     05   Orlando.   (= (1) with more context)
(24) "I'll see you in the morning." She laughed. "*I mean*, afternoon."
                                          (FLOB[6] quoted from Brinton 2008: 115)

While *I mean* in examples (23) and (24) may be replaced by utterances such as *No, that's not true*, the following example may be replaced by statements such as *to be more precise*.

(25) JA: Do Isabella and Connor come down to Nashville a lot?
     NK: No, they don't. They're not crazy about Nashville. They're so
         grown up now. *I mean*, they're adults.   (COCA)

Example (25) is an excerpt from an interview between two famous Hollywood actresses. JA is the host and NK is the guest, and JA is asking about NK's children. NK says that her children are not interested in visiting Nashville and when giving the reason, she uses the phrase *grown up* but then replaces it with *adults*. According to my native-English-speaker informants, *they're grown up* means (or gives an impression) that *they* (NK's children) are mentally adults while not necessarily being adults from a legal perspective. The expression *adults*, on the other hand, refers strictly to those who are legally, mentally, and physically mature. Therefore, the speaker appears to have used *I mean* because the first phrase she used did not exactly convey what she wanted to express. In the preceding examples, the speaker fails to follow the Maxim of Manner in the previous discourse as her statement contains ambiguity, but does obey the maxim after *I mean*.

The uses of *I mean* in examples (23) through (25) occur at the what-is-said level, since the speakers use *I mean* to refer to the relation of the propositional content, such as *in the afternoon not morning*, and *adults rather than grown up*.[7]

4.2.3 *I mean* at the Implicature Level

A violation of Grice's Maxims is also observed at the implicature level. Speakers correct or clarify what is implicated at this level. It may sound odd that an implicature could be misconveyed, since it is the speaker who generates it.

However, as exemplified below, even though speakers have intentions to be conveyed, speakers sometimes avoid stating them clearly and risk the hearer's misconception of their intentions. *I mean* indicates that an implicature generated in the previous discourse is not what the speaker intended to convey to the hearer. Below is an example showing a violation of the Maxim of Quantity before *I mean* at the level of implicature. In (26), there are three participants, A, B, and C, and utterances B and B' are the two different answers to A's question.

(26)   A: Have you guys been to Australia before?
          B: He has. *I mean*, I'm going to visit there next year though.
          B': I haven't. *I mean*, I'm going to visit there next year though.
(27)   a. He has.
          b. +> I have not been to Australia

As shown in (27b), speaker B implicates PCI that he has not been to Australia by mentioning C (=*He* in example (26)) but not himself. The speaker provides less information than required. While the purpose of flouting the Maxim of Quantity is generally to avoid explicit or negative statements, speaker B uses *I mean* to show that the implicature resulting from flouting the Maxim of Quantity is not what he intended to convey. Conversely, in answer B', the speaker observes the Maxim of Quantity by mentioning himself. According to native speakers of English, answer B' sounds like it could have been uttered by those who overuse fillers. Their comments go on to indicate that other discourse markers can also be used in this context and *I mean* in answer B' is less likely to be said in the first place. Therefore, it can be said that answer B' with no violation of a maxim is not the core usage of *I mean* in terms of Grice's Conversational Maxims. The following example shows the GCI generated by observing the Maxim of Quantity:

(28)   01 R: Yeah. It's like – it's probably about six to Penn and it's
          02   about eight to D.C., and four to New York – little less than
          03   four to New York. There are buses – like two other buses
          04   that's about 15 dollars. If you get them really early, you
          05   can get it for a dollar.
          06 T: Really?
          07 R: To New York.
          08 T: Like early like?
          09 R: Like two months early I mean or, and early in the morning.
          10   It's like you have to do both. *I mean*, even if you don't do
          11   that, you can do like 10 dollars to 15 dollars.   (CRMTP 17)

(29) a. It's like you have to do both.
b. +> You cannot get a cheap bus ticket unless you fulfill the condition: book an early-morning bus two month earlier

In (28), R and T are talking about buses between Boston and other cities. In lines 01–04, R mentions the duration and the fare of the bus ride. R, who is a senior to T, also explains how to get cheaper tickets. From Line 09 onward, R advises booking an early-morning bus two months prior to the scheduled departure. In terms of Grice's Conversational Maxims, when the speaker says, *you have to do both*, the hearer infers (29b) by presupposing that the speaker follows the Maxim of Quantity and that the speaker implicates that both conditions of early-morning bus and early booking enable him to obtain a cheaper ticket. The speaker then uses *I mean* in line 10 to indicate that the implicature generated in the previous discourse is not exactly what the speaker wants to convey. As the implicature is not the speaker's true belief, the use of *I mean* can be said to have occurred at implicature level.

In the following example, the speaker uses *I mean* to refer to the implicature generated by observing the Maxim of Quality.

(30) JEREMY: I remember seeing a picture of him before. I was going through some old photographs, cleaning out a closet. Amy said it was an old boyfriend.
BOOTH: Hmm. They keep in contact?
JEREMY: No. *I mean*, uh, she would have told me. Why? You don't think that – did he kill her?   (*Bones*, 2005/ 9- TV series)

(31) a. No.
b. +> The speaker believes that his wife and her old boyfriend did not keep in contact and has sufficient evidence that she did not

The conversation above is between FBI agent Booth and the suspect, Jeremy. In his murder investigation, Booth asks the suspect if the victim, Amy (Jeremy's wife), was in contact with her old boyfriend. Jeremy first answers *No* and then adds the reason why he believes this is so. Grice's CP and strict observation of the Maxim of Quality lead to the GCI that the speaker has concrete evidence for his assertion, as seen in (31b). If this were the speaker's true intention, he would not have used *I mean*. By *I mean*, the speaker shows that the implicature is not what he wants to convey. Therefore, here it can also be said that the speaker has violated the Maxim of Quality at the implicature level. The two utterances *No* and *she would have told me* are not connected with the causal relationship, but the speaker merely provides one reason why he believes this is so (See example (49) for more detail about the relation types).

The implicature in the following example arises through the speaker's flouting of the Maxim of Relation.

(32) DOYLEY: Last time I found him, he was, um, signed on to a Liberian Oil tanker bound for Tibet del Fuego.
ANGELA: Oh, okay. That narrows it down. He's a sailor, he's maybe Brazilian, and he's named after a flute.
HODGINS: You, you know what else narrows it down. He's a titan – half man, half god. *I mean*, I can see why ... why you've ...
ANGELA: Hodgins, stop it. (*Bones*, 2005/ 9- TV series)

(33) a. He's a titan – half man, half god.
b. +> I am insulting the guy you once married

Angela and Hodgins in (32) are thinking about marriage, but it turns out that she was once married to another man, and she does not even remember if her marriage is still valid. For Angela and Hodgins to get married, they have to find the man to finalize the divorce. Doyley, the detective hired by Angela, learns that the man is a sailor, probably a Brazilian, and is named after a flute. In (32) before *I mean*, Hodgins talks nonsense about the man being a god, but then says after *I mean* that he understands why Angela married him. The speaker, by his statement (33a), flouts the Maxim of Relation since not factually true. The PCI would be (33b), first, because Hodgins sometimes teases people for fun. Secondly because Hodgins is being in shock after Angela turned out to have been married without remembering it. He realizes that the implicature is not what he wanted to convey and uses *I mean* to obey the maxim. After *I mean*, the speaker follows the Maxim of Quality and attempts to say that he understands why Angela has been married to the man.

The following examples are cases in which the speaker flouts the Maxim of Manner:

(34) Jesse: I don't hate you, all right? Come on, it's no big deal, all right? I flew all the way over there, you blew the thing off, and then my life has been a big nosedive since then, but *I mean* it's not a problem.
Céline: No, you can't say that!
Jesse: No, I'm kidding, I'm kidding. (*Before Sunset*, 2004/ 7 movie)

(35) a. I don't hate you, all right? Come on, it's no big deal, all right? I flew all the way over there, you blew the thing off, and then my life has been a big nosedive since then.
b. +> It was a big deal

Jesse, a young American man, and Céline, a French woman, promised when they first met to have a reunion in half a year. However, Céline could not make it because of her grandmother's funeral. The conversation in (34) takes place in Paris nine years after they made that promise, when Jesse accused Céline of not showing up as planned. Before *I mean*, Jesse flouts the Maxim of Manner implicating that what she has done was really a terrible thing (= (35b)). Nevertheless, as shown in the utterance after *I mean*, his purpose is not to blame her but to make use of the effect of the implicature. The speaker's use of *I mean* can be explained as follows: He flouts the Maxim of Manner so as to induce the effect of redundancy, then he uses *I mean* to show that it is not his true intention. The following example shows GCI generated by observing the Maxim of Manner.

(36) Patrick: Takashi and Hanna came to LA to see me. *I mean*, not together because they don't hang out anymore.
(37) a. Takashi and Hanna came to LA to see me.
  b. +> Takashi and Hanna came to LA together.

In (36), by the connective *and*, the speaker generates the GCI (37b) that Takashi and Hanna visited the speaker's place together by observing the Maxim of Manner. Then he uses *I mean* to indicate that the GCI is not what the speaker wanted to convey.

With respect to Grice's CP and the four maxims, *I mean* marks a speaker's failure to obey the Maxim of Quality (or Manner) at either the what-is-said level or implicature level in the preceding discourse, as well as the intention to obey the maxim in the following utterance. The motivations for using *I mean* are thus illustrated as in Table 4.1.

	Previous Utterance	*I mean*	Following Utterance
What-is-said Level	The speaker does not follow the Maxim of Quality or Manner	Marks an offense of the Grice's Maxim of Quality (i.e., what is said or implicated is not what the speaker wants to convey) and the speaker's will to follow the maxim	The speaker follows the Maxim of Quality (or Manner)
Implicature Level	The implicature generated by observing or exploiting the Maxim of Quantity, Quality, Relation, or Manner		

Table 4.1: The usages of *I mean* at the what-is-said level and implicature level

4.3 Analysis from Politeness Theory

Our analysis based on Grice's CP and the four maxims provided an account for why speakers use *I mean*. However, motivations for using it are not limited to what is said or implicated in the previous utterance. See the example below:

(38)   "Yes, but sir..."
"Yes, Willoughby?"
The CO's smile was really very pleasant.
"It's what you joined to do, isn't it?"
"No, sir. *I mean* Yes, sir. I mean, I'm an actor, sir."
He gulped and went rushing on.
"I have to start rehearsal on Monday, I've got a new job to go back to."
(BNC)[8]

This conversation takes place at a military cocktail party. The commanding officer (CO) is telling Willoughby to go to the front line. Asking about his reason for joining the military, Willoughby first responds *No sir*, which is his honest answer, although he replaced it with *Yes, sir*, a more respectful and appropriate answer to the CO in military. In (38), because Willoughby's answer *No, sir* is fully truthful, the speaker follows the Maxim of Quality on both the what-is-said and implicature levels. This example cannot be explained by Grice's Maxims, but by Politeness Theory. In short, the speaker uses *I mean* in order to save the hearer's face.

4.3.1 Politeness Theory

According to Brown and Levinson (1987), "politeness" is a particular pattern (or convergence) of motives for deviations from the rational and efficient communication described in Grice's works:

> The convergence is remarkable because, on the face of it, the usages are irrational: the convergence is in the particular *divergences* from some highly rational maximally efficient mode of communication (as, for example, outlined by Grice 1967, 1975). We isolate a motive – politeness, very broadly and specially defined – and then claim, paradoxically enough, that the only satisfactory explanatory scheme will include a heavy dash of rationalism.   (ibid. 55)

Their theory, which I call Politeness Theory in this book, focuses on interpersonal relationships in culture and society. Among their key concepts is "face," which consists of two fundamental human desires.

> **negative face:** the want of every 'competent adult member' that his actions be unimpeded by others

positive face: the want of every member that his wants be desirable to at least some others (ibid. 62)

Those are basic desires both of which people wish to satisfy in conversation. The former is the desire not to be interrupted by others (which only adult members of society possess), and the latter is the desire to be well thought of by others (which every member of society possesses). "Politeness" is the speaker's consideration of what expression to choose to save face in a given situation. Strategies to protect the addressee's negative face from being threatened are called "negative politeness" and the one to save the addressee's positive face is called "positive politeness." Brown and Levinson identify 10 negative and 15 positive politeness strategies.

Negative Politeness Strategies
1. Be conventionally indirect
2. Question, hedge
3. Be pessimistic
4. Minimize the imposition, R_x
5. Give deference
6. Apologize
7. Impersonalize S and H: Avoid the pronouns 'I' and 'you'
8. State the FTA as a general rule
9. Nominalize
10. Go on record as incurring a debt, or as not indebting H (ibid. 131)

In English the second member of pairs like Snuggs/Dr Snuggs, eat/dine, man/gentleman, give/bestow, bit/piece, book/volume and so on encode greater respect to the person, activity or thing. (ibid. 181)

As shown above, the expression *Dr. Snuggs* is less face-threatening than just *Snuggs*. Among the positive politeness strategies are "Notice, attend to H" and "Avoid disagreement":[9]

Positive Politeness Strategies
1. Notice, attend to H (his interests, wants, needs, goods)
2. Exaggerate (interest, approval, sympathy with H)
3. Intensify interest to H
4. Use in-group identity markers
5. Seek agreement
6. Avoid disagreement
7. Presuppose/raise/assert/common ground

8. Joke
9. Assert or presuppose S's knowledge of and concern for H's wants
10. Offer, promise
11. Be optimistic
12. Include both S and H in the activity
13. Give (or ask for) reasons
14. Assume or assert reciprocity
15. Give gifts to H (goods, sympathy, understanding, cooperation)

(ibid. 102)

As the example below shows, when a speaker makes a request of an addressee that potentially threatens the addressee's NF, the speaker can ensure PF for the addressee by commenting on a personal detail, which also helps to ameliorate the degree of the possible threat to face:

(39) *'Goodness, you cut your hair!'* (...) By the way, I came to borrow some flour. (ibid. 103)

Some types of speech acts inevitably threaten either the speaker's or hearer's face, and conversational participants use politeness strategies to reduce the degree of the threat. Such speech acts are called Face-Threatening Acts (FTAs).

	negative face	*positive face*
threaten S	promises	apologies
threaten H	warnings	criticisms

Table 4.2: The relationship between the speech-act type and threats to face

(Ibid. 286)

For example, apologies threaten a speaker's PF by forcing the speaker to admit that he had done something wrong or uncomfortable to the hearer.

4.3.2 *I mean* to Save Hearer's Negative Face

When the motivation for using *I mean* does not involve Grice's conversational implicatures, it instead involves face-saving in Politeness Theory. Examples (40) through (42) show *I mean* used to redress the threat to the hearer's NF in the previous utterance:

(40) "Hi, Damian!" Tony smiled, then did a double take at the look in Damian's knife-like eyes. "I — *I mean* Mr. Flint"; he amended hurriedly and extended a hand. "How are you, sir?" (BNC)

For example, in (40), the speaker uses *I mean* to redress the threat to the hearer's NF. Tony calls Damian by his first name at first, but Damian, who he considers his rival in love, gives him a sharp glance. Feeling intense displeasure from Damian, Tony addresses him more formally. As Damian and Mr. Flint are the same person, this *I mean* operates not on the level of what is said nor on the level of implicature; the speaker satisfies all of Grice's Maxims in his previous discourse. Instead, the speaker's consideration of the hearer's antipathy motivates the speaker to use *I mean*.

In terms of Politeness Theory, this can be explained as follows: The speaker first attempts to save the hearer's PF by addressing him casually but this instead threatens the hearer's negative face. Thus, after *I mean*, the speaker manages to save the hearer's negative face. Also in the next two examples, speakers use *I mean* in order to redress the threat to the hearer's NF:

(41) PROF ENO: That's enough! It does appear to be a poem, though. Hmmm... "time to die, you stupid bald git. Your conceptual ambient albums don't mean shit/ Your teaching methods of meaning are bereft. And Roxy Music were only good when you left." Is this about me, by any chance?
ICE-T: Yes, *I mean*, no! It's about ... Erm... it's about George Bush.
PROF ENO: I see. And is that why it's called "Teacher Killer"? (BNC)

In (41), the British musician Eno teaches music to American hip-hop singers. ICE-T, one of the students there, writes these lyrics for a class assignment, and Eno wants to confirm that they are not about him. ICE-T first admits this saying *Yes* but then he changes his mind (probably because he saw Eno's face), saying *No! It's about George Bush*. It is obvious that Eno does not like ICE-T's first answer. In this example, the speaker as a student thus tries to redress the threat to NF of the hearer as a teacher by replacing *Yes* with *No* using *I mean*. The following example can also be explained as saving the hearer's NF in that the utterance before *I mean*, *No, sir* is not a respectful reply to a command officer (CO) in military. Confirming that fighting at the front line is what the soldier (named Willoughby) joined to do, the CO expects an answer *Yes, sir*. However, Willoughby answered honestly, which threatens the hearer's NF. He then replaces his answer with *No, sir* so as to meet the CO's expectation:

(42) The CO's smile was really very pleasant.
"It's what you joined to do, isn't it?"
"No, sir. *I mean* Yes, sir. I mean, I'm an actor, sir." (Excerpt from (37))

As shown in examples above, speakers use *I mean* when they have threatened the hearer's NF in the previous discourse. Then after *I mean*, they redress the threat or save face. Therefore, in the cases above, *I mean* marks both these threats to and also the desire to save face afterwards.

4.3.3 *I mean* to Save Speaker's and Hearer's Positive Face

When correcting an obvious misstatement on the what-is-said level, I, a native Japanese speaker, always add an expression of apology, such as *Oh, I'm sorry* or *Oh, that's wrong*, before such a correction. It has taken me a long time to get used to using only *I mean* without such an accompanying expression of apology. However, depending on the addressee, whom native English speakers also preface *I mean* with an apology, as in *(I'm) Sorry, I mean* in certain contexts:

(43) a. (to a stranger)
Excuse me, may I borrow your pen? **I'm sorry,** *I mean* a pencil.
b. (to a stranger)
Excuse me, may I borrow your pen? *I mean* a pencil.
c. (to your close friend)
Hey, can I borrow your pen? *I mean* a pencil.
d. (to your close friend)
Hey, can I borrow your pen? **I'm sorry,** *I mean* a pencil.

(44) a. A professor: What time is your appointment?
A student: I'm afraid it's at 2 o'clock today ... **I'm sorry,** *I mean* it's at 3.
b. A professor: What time is your appointment?
A student: I'm afraid it's at 2 o'clock today ... *I mean* it's at 3.
c. (between friends)
A: What time is the Celtics' game tonight?
B: From 7, *I mean* it's from 8.
d. (between friends)
A: What time is the Celtics' game tonight?
B: From 7, **I'm sorry,** *I mean* it's from 8.

Examples (43) and (44) compare *I mean* with and without an apology in two different situations. According to native English speakers, in both of these examples, (a) and (c) are more natural or appropriate than (b) and (d). Thus, for those who are socially distant, the speaker is expected to insert an expression of apology, but for those with whom one is socially intimate, this is not necessary. From the perspective of Politeness Theory, the speaker uses Negative

Politeness Strategy No.6 in correcting the misstatements in (43a) and (44a). By apologizing, the speaker can save the hearer's negative face, although his own PF is threatened (see Table 4.2). On the other hand, in (43c) and (44c), the speaker corrects his misstatement without an apology so saves his own PF (or prevents it from being threatened) by using *I mean*. The characteristic of saving speaker's face is shared by all usages of *I mean* without an apology.[10]

To describe *I mean* as a marker to save the speaker's own PF may sound negative, but it turns out that it also serves to save the hearer's PF as well. According to informants, the reason *I mean* without a preceding apology sounds more natural and appropriate is that apologies are simply not required for such small mistakes in casual conversation. Therefore, as seen in (43c) and (44c), what the speaker is concerned about is not the hearer's NF (and probably not the speaker's PF), but rather the hearer's PF, much like the utterance such as *Do not mention it between us*. Apologizing in such a situation, on the contrary, could lead to an ironic interpretation, as in the following examples:

(45) How is your husband doing? *I'M SORRY, I MEAN* your EX-husband.[11]
(46) Well, I guess it doesn't matter. If the cop-killer (oops, *sorry – I mean* the young gentleman) is convicted in his second trial, I'm sure they'll sentence him to a "time-out." (COCA)

In PDE corpora, *I mean* rarely co-occurs with *(I'm) Sorry*.

	(I'm) Sorry I mean	Total of *I mean*	Rate
BNC	5	24223	0.0002%
COCA	42	111002	0.0004%

Table 4.3: Token frequency of *(I'm) Sorry I mean* in PDE corpora

It is much more common for English speakers to use *I mean* without an expression of apology. This is not only because the speaker wants to avoid an apology or save the speaker's face, but to save the hearer's PF.

Politeness Theory thus provides another motivation for using *I mean*: to save the hearer's PF. This transcends the levels of what is said (i.e., the metalinguistic level) and implicature (i.e., the mental level) and represents the social level (which I call the Face Level). *I mean* marks both potential threats to the hearer's face and a speaker's will to redress the threat in the discourse to follow. In addition, correcting wrong information with *I mean* but without an apology saves the speaker's or hearer's PF.

4.4 Summary

In this chapter, two pragmatic theories, Grice's Conversational Principle and four maxims and Brown and Levinson's Politeness Theory, were used to account for speaker motivation to use *I mean*. Speakers use *I mean* for one or more of the following reasons in the previous discourse:

(i) The speaker does not follow one of Grice's Maxims at What-is-said Level,
(ii) the speaker does not follow one of Grice's Maxims at Implicature Level, or
(iii) the speaker threatens the hearer's negative face.

I mean also marks a speaker's intention to obey the Maxim of Quality or to redress the face threat in the discourse. Moreover, the fact that a speaker can use *I mean* without apologizing allows a speaker to save his own face and that of the hearer.

The pragmatic account of *I mean* can thus be summarized in Table 4.4.

	Previous Utterance	*I mean*	Following Utterance
What-is-said Level	The speaker does not follow a maxim in propositional content	Marks an offense of the Grice's Maxim of Quality (i.e., what is said or implicated is not what the speaker wants to convey) and the speaker's will to follow the maxim	The speaker follows the Maxim of Quality (or Manner)
Implicature Level	The implicature generated by observing or exploiting the Maxim of Quantity, Quality, Relation, or Manner		
Face Level	The speaker threatens the hearer's NF	Marks a threat of face and the speaker's will to redress the threat	The speaker redresses the threat
	The speaker saves his own or the hearer's PF		

Table 4.4: A pragmatic account of the motivation for using *I mean*

Notes

1 Markkanen (1985) also mentions the relation between the use of *I mean* and Grice's Conversational Maxims and notes that *I mean* is a hedge expression associated with Grice's Maxims of Quantity and Manner, since it shows more precise and correct information is to follow.

I mean could be included in the hedges on either the Maxim of Quantity or the Maxim of Manner since it seems to signal that previous information was not precise enough or not altogether correct and that more precise or more correct information is to follow ... .

(ibid. 59)

The preceding statement captures only one (albeit important) aspect of *I mean* with respect to Grice's Conversational Maxims. However, replacing imprecise or incorrect information with that which is precise or correct happens at the what-is-said level. Furthermore, a speaker replaces information at the implicature level motivated by an (intentional or unintentional) offense of one of the four maxims; this is discussed in a subsequent section in this chapter.

2 Note that the issue of whether conversational implicature is a part of speaker meaning or pragmatic inference has sparked recent controversy. Saul (2002) and Horn (2009) support the former, while Sperber and Wilson (1986) and Levinson (2000) support the latter (Huang 2014: 33n). This book adopts the former position rather than the latter, since the speaker's motivation for using *I mean* is ascribed to the SPEAKER's assumption of the hearer's assumption (i.e., what the speaker knows or thinks about the hearer at the time of the speech, not what the hearer really knows or thinks analyzed from researcher's objective point of view).

3 Quotations on the Cooperative Principle and the four maxims are from Grice (1989: 26–27).

4 Grice outlines four cases in which speakers do not follow the maxims: speakers violate it, opt out of it, flout it, or two maxims impose contradictory requirements. He describes them as follows.

> A participant in a talk exchange may fail to fulfill a maxim in various ways, which include the following:
> 1. He may quietly and unostentatiously VIOLATE a maxim; if so, in some cases he will be liable to mislead.
> 2. He may OPT OUT from the operation both of the maxim and of the CP; he may say, indicate, or allow it to become plain that he is unwilling to cooperate in the way the maxim requires. He may say, for example, *I cannot say more; my lips are sealed*.
> 3. He may be faced by a CLASH: He may be unable, for example, to fulfill the first maxim of Quantity (Be as informative as is required) without violating the second maxim of Quality (Have adequate evidence for what you say).
> 4. He may FLOUT a maxim; that is, he may BLATANTLY fail to fulfill it.   (ibid. 49)

The crucial factor differentiating the "generalized conversational implicature" and "particularized conversational implicature" is that the former is context independent and the latter is context dependent. For example, in the case of (19), the utterance *He has (been to Australia)* usually means the referent *he* went to Australia, but does not entail that the actual speaker has not been there. The implicature of the speaker's not having visited Australia can only be generated in this specific context.

5 The representation "+>" stands for "conversationally implicate."
6 Freiburg-LOB Corpus
7 The process of how implicatures are generated can also be adapted to the what-is-said level. Levinson (2000) wrote:

> Grice's account makes implicature dependent on a prior determination of the "the said." The said in turn depends on disambiguation, indexical resolution, reference fixing, ... But each of these processes, which are prerequisites to determining the proposition expressed, may themselves depend crucially on processes that look indistinguishable from implicatures. Thus what is said seems both to determine and to be determined by implicature.   (ibid. 186)

Levinson dubbed this process "Grice's circle" and stated that it is the greatest challenge to any theory seeking to define the border between semantics and pragmatics. Given that there is no clear border between them (which is equivalent to the tenet of cognitive linguistics (Langacker 2008: 40–41)).

8 British National Corpus (http://bnc.jkn21.com)
9 S and H in capitals stand for speaker and hearer respectively.

10 Fukuhara (2010) argues that PF and NF can be further classified into two more categories for each.
> PF+ [Plus Characteristics]:
> > S wants to be understood and be a friend.
>
> PF– [Minus Characteristics]:
> > S does not want to be criticized and hated.
>
> NF+ [Plus Characteristics]:
> > S wants to be free and independent.
>
> NF– [Minus Characteristics]:
> > S does not want to be restricted and forced to do something.
>
> (ibid. 161, originally in Japanese)

He noted that the Japanese sentence-final expression "zyan" acquired a usage only to save speaker's PF+. Speakers save his own PF+ with "zyan" because they present their personal information as if it is a common knowledge, which makes it difficult for hearers to offer a counterargument. In the case of *I mean*, the speaker uses it to redress the threat to speaker's NF–. Using *I mean* itself has an effect to save speaker's PF– or hearer's PF+.

11 Prosodic emphases are marked with small capital letters.

CHAPTER 5
A Cognitive Linguistic Account of *I mean*

5.1 Introduction

Previous studies have defined *I mean* as a marker of modification (e.g., Schiffrin 1987; Fox Tree and Schrock 2002) and classified the usages according to the kind of information appearing before and after *I mean*. However, we have not yet examined the primary motivation for using *I mean* that explain all the uses thereof. This chapter looks more carefully into the hidden cognitive process behind the modification by *I mean* and aims to account for the question of why speakers use *I mean* and how its usages are related.

In the previous chapter, pragmatic theories, Grice's Conversational Maxims and Politeness Theory, describe speaker motivation as the speaker's violation of Grice's Maxims, either at a what-is-said or implicature level, or as a threat to the hearer's face. It seems reasonable to assume that conversational participants are cooperative by nature, since sufficient evidence from the latest developmental psychology research shows that cooperativeness is a unique characteristic of human communication (cf. Tomasello 2008), and *I mean* functions as an adjustment in such a conversation (Fox Tree and Schrock 2002). Although pragmatic accounts have unveiled various discourse functions of *I mean*, their descriptive tradition does not address the roots of its use. Hence, different pragmatic theories are required to explain how a particular linguistic element works at various discourse levels; propositional content level, face level, or other interpersonal levels. This chapter explains all the usages of *I mean* and their relationships from the perspective of a single theory, cognitive grammar (CG). The motivation for using *I mean* and the relations among the usages can be attributed to the basic human cognitive ability of "intersubjectivity", and the cognitive process behind the speaker's use of *I mean* can be illustrated by a modified version of Current Discourse Space (CDS).

5.2 The Basic Tenet of Cognitive Linguistics

In cognitive linguistics, linguistic meaning is considered "conceptualization." In other words, it implies how we, as agents of cognition ("conceptualizer"), construe the surrounding world through basic human cognitive concepts (e.g., categorization, specificity, and reference point) and how this reflects on linguistic meaning. Moreover, traditional and exclusive categories, such as morphology, lexicon, grammar (or syntax), and pragmatics, are not isolated but connected to each other through the formation of sequences.

> Starting from single words, ... The next level is **discourse**, where any number of sentences ... are connected to form a coherent linguistic production ..., Although discourse is often considered a separate topic, ... the contrast with lower levels is at most a matter of degree.
>
> (Langacker 2008: 457)

The structure of discourse is not a mere collective total of lexicons, phrases, and clauses; it constitutes an integrated conceptualization that continuously updates itself along the flow of discourse (see Figure 5.1).

> Discourse is not just a sequence of words, clauses, or sentences. It is also – and more essentially – a series of conceptions associated with these forms. ..., each develops from and builds on the previous one, so as discourse proceeds an integrated conceptual structure of progressively greater complexity is being constructed.
>
> (ibid. 486)

Previous Discourse	Current Discourse	Anticipated Discourse
Conceptualization1	[Conceptualization1]	
	Conceptualization2	[Conceptualization2]
		Conceptualization3

Time ⟶

Figure 5.1: The formation of integrated conceptualization

As the preceding passages note, in CG, no explicit boundary is established between lexicon and grammar, nor between discourse, semantics, or pragmatics. They are all connected and form a gradation.

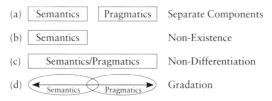

Figure 5.2: The cognitive linguistic model of the relationship between semantics and pragmatics (Ibid. 40)

The claim, instead, is that semantics and pragmatics form a gradation, as shown in (d), with no precise boundary between the two. But toward either extreme of the scale lie phenomena that are indisputably either semantic or pragmatic. (ibid. 40)

This study thus considers all usages of *I mean* to form a gradation. The usages differ in both their semantic or pragmatic scale and the discourse level at which they function.

5.3 Relevant Notions of Cognitive Linguistics

5.3.1 Profiling

The "profile" is the limited area of the cognitive field in our focus when we verbalize a certain object. For example, the meanings of the words "arc," "roof," "husband," and "wife" are the focused parts of the whole. The focused part constitutes the profile, while the unfocused whole is called the "base." In cognitive linguistics, linguistic meaning is also defined as a profile on a base. The profile is illustrated by the bold line in the diagram below.

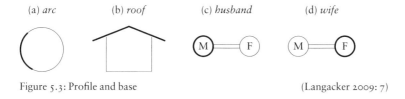

Figure 5.3: Profile and base (Langacker 2009: 7)

In these examples, the meanings of "arc" and "roof" are described as focused part of the whole: a curve of the entire circle and an upper part of the entire house. "Husband" and "wife" are also the focused part of the whole, where the relationship of "married couple" needs to evoke.

5.3.2 Construal

The definition of linguistic meaning as conceptualization is the most fundamental notion in cognitive linguistics. The notion of conceptualization corresponds to "construal," which means the way in which conceptualizers physically and mentally view the world. Construal includes "specificity," "focusing," "prominence," and "perspective." Specificity refers to precision in describing an object. The examples (47a) through (47c) list expressions describing the same situations from low specificity (high schematicity) to high specificity (low schematicity):

(47) a. rodent → rat → large brown rat → large brown rat with halitosis
b. thing → object → tool → hammer → claw hammer
c. Something happened. → A person perceived a rodent. → A girl saw a porcupine. → An alert little girl wearing glasses caught a brief glimpse of a ferocious porcupine with sharp quills.

(Langacker 2008: 56)

Perspective refers to the conceptualizer's viewpoint, which is crucial for the meaning of certain linguistic expressions, as the following examples show.

(48) a. The hill gently rises from the bank of the river.
b. The hill gently falls to the bank of the river. (Langacker 2008: 82)

The speakers in (48a) and (48b) observe the same objective scene, although their vantage points are different: the bottom of the hill in (48a) and the top of the hill in (48b). The two sentences could have been uttered either physically in front of the hill or in front of a picture of the hill. However, in both cases, the conceptualizer's perspective determines whether the hill rises or falls, not the hill itself. Such shifts in the conceptualizer's perspective are called "mental scanning."

5.3.3 Reference Point Relationship

When we verbalize, the verbalized entity is the conceptualizer's focus in the field of cognition, and the focused entity is the profile. The entity that is to be profiled, however, is not always easily accessible physically or mentally. In that case, the conceptualizer first contacts the entity with high prominence and easier accessibility and subsequently reaches for the entity to be profiled. For example, when one wants to access a car that is owned by John, one has to access John, the owner, first and then the car (as in the expression *John's car*). The cognitive ability enabling us to use prominent entities as stepping stones to entities with low accessibility is "reference point ability" (cf. Langacker 1999: 173). The stepping stone is called the "reference point" (e.g., *John*), and the goal of the mental access is called the "target" (e.g., *car*). The relationship between the reference point and the target is known as the "reference point relationship," which can be illustrated as in Figure 5.4 below:

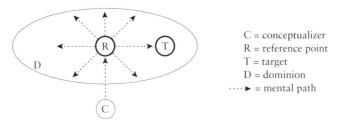

C = conceptualizer
R = reference point
T = target
D = dominion
----▶ = mental path

Figure 5.4: Reference point relationship   (Langacker 2008: 84)

"Dominion" represents the assembly of what is accessible to the conceptualizer (C), and the arrows pointing in all directions represent reference points, which indicate that the conceptualizer has access to any entity within the dominion. The dotted arrows represent the process of mental scanning, which constitutes a "mental path."

5.3.4 Grounding

"Grounding" is a function specific to some specific linguistic expressions. It relates the "ground" (where the actual speaker and hearer exist) to the profiled entity. In other words, grounding functions as a reference point relationship, with the ground as a reference point and the profiled entity as a target. There are two types of the grounding systems: nominal grounding and clausal grounding. The former identifies and specifies the identity of objects, while the latter represents the existence of a profiled process with respect to the ground (i.e., it shows whether or not the event has occurred, how the occurrence is related to the ground (for example, when it occurs), and how the occurrence is construed by the conceptualizer). Linguistic elements functioning as a part of the process of grounding are called the "grounding elements." Articles and demonstratives are typical elements of nominal grounding, while tenses and modals are typical of clausal grounding. For example, the indefinite article *a/an* designates an entity that is unspecified between the speaker and the hearer, while the definite article *the* designates an entity that is specified between them. The two types of grounding are represented in Figure 5.5.

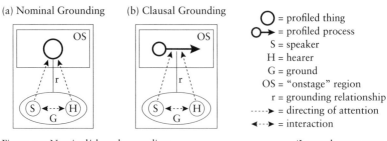

Figure 5.5: Nominal/clausal grounding (Langacker 2009: 150)

Figure 5.5 (a) and (b) shows an entity profiled on the "onstage region,"[1] the grounding relationship between the entity and the ground, and the joint attention of the two conceptualizers in the ground. What differentiates nominal from clausal grounding is the profiled entity: the former profiles a thing, and the latter a process.

5.3.5 Intersubjectivity

This book mainly refers to the approach of Verhagen (2007) toward intersubjectivity and develops a discussion based on the notion of "subjectivity." The current usages of *I mean* can be categorized as a process of "subjectification."

Verhagen (2007) focused on cognitive processes that reflect both the speaker's and hearer's perspectives so that two conceptualizers (conceptualizer1 and conceptualizer2), namely the speaker and hearer in a conversation, are always depicted in a basic construal configuration.

Object of conceptualization:

Subject of conceptualization (Ground):

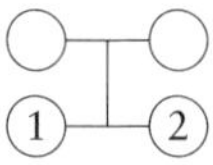

Figure 5.6: The basic construal configuration (Verhagen 2007: 60)

The two circles at the bottom represent two conceptualizers, and the two circles and the horizontal line connecting them represent the object of construal. The vertical line connecting the two schematic representations of the object and subject of conceptualizations correspond to construal or the joint attention of the two conceptualizers. Common nouns such as *lamp* and *Bathroom* on a doorplate, for example, objectively represent themselves what they are, while conceptualizer's construal process is hardly relevant. As shown in Figure 5.7, only elements at the level of the object of conceptualization are profiled in terms of their conceptualizations. In contrast, interjections (such as greetings such as *Hi!* and expressions of apology such as *Sorry*) do not describe the

CHAPTER 5   A COGNITIVE LINGUISTIC ACCOUNT OF *I MEAN*   59

objective world. Furthermore, the construal process by which the conceptualizers construe the object plays no role in their conceptualizations. Their meanings are designated only in the relationship between the two conceptualizers. Hence, as shown in Figure 5.8, only the elements at the ground level are profiled.

Object of conceptualization:
Subject of conceptualization (Ground):

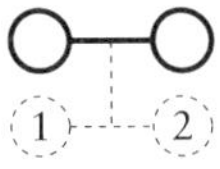

Figure 5.7: Maximally objective construal configuration   (Ibid. 61)

Object of conceptualization:
Subject of conceptualization (Ground):

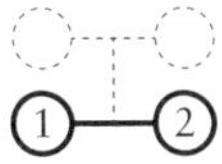

Figure 5.8: Highly subjective construal configuration   (Ibid. 62)

The expressions shown above such as *lump* and *Hi!* reflect extreme patterns of cognitive processes, while the typical daily expressions lie in between a maximally objective construal and a highly subjective construal:

> Labeling objects and producing interjections constitute the opposite extremes on a continuum from maximally objective to maximally subjective expressions, and thus the exceptions; expressions in the "middle part" of this continuum are the rule.   (ibid. 62)

Verhagen (2007) emphasized the "coordination relationship," which is the adjustment or negotiation of information between the speaker and hearer in an attempt to create a common ground. This relationship is the equivalent of intersubjectivity and is directly motivated by the cognitive ability to take another person's perspective:

> I have furthermore suggested that the basic construal configuration should be seen as involving a relation of intersubjective coordination, reflecting the typically human cognitive ability to identify with conspecifics, and thus to conceive of things from other points of view.   (ibid.62)

> The relevant dimension here is defined by the specific human ability to entertain other points of view in the same way as one's own, which we explicitly incorporated into the construal configuration by distinguishing two subjects of conceptualization.   (ibid. 67)

Intersubjective coordination is illustrated by a horizontal line that connects the two conceptualizers in configurations.

In the process of diachronic semantic development or extensions in synchronic usages, some expressions show a shift in profile from more profiled elements of the object of conceptualization to more profiled elements of the subject of conceptualization. This profile shift phenomenon is called "subjectification":

> ... subjectification may involve an expression initially profiling no part of the ground or not profiling the construal relationship and then acquiring the potential of profiling, ... the construal relationship and/or parts of the ground. ..., the differences and changes can all be construed as "shifts" in the degree of profiling of elements and relations in the basic construal configuration. (ibid. 73-76)

Verhagen (2007) cited that the expression *I think* functions both as a matrix clause and an epistemic marker. The difference between its two usages can be illustrated as follows; Figure 5.9 represents the former and Figure 5.10 represents the latter:

Object of conceptualization:
Subject of conceptualization (Ground):

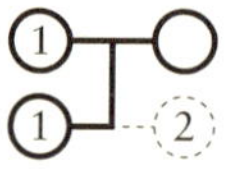

Figure 5.9: *I think* as a matrix clause (Ibid. 71)

Object of conceptualization:
Subject of conceptualization (Ground):

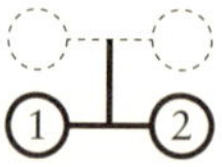

Figure 5.10: *I think* as an epistemic marker (Ibid. 69)

The profile of the vertical line and the number *1* in the top circle in Figure 5.9 show the speaker's epistemic attitude toward the propositional content. Both the propositional content and the speaker himself are onstage (i.e., the speaker and his construal are objectively construed). In Figure 5.10, on the other hand, no element of the object of conceptualization is profiled because the speaker is subjectively construed, and the speaker's epistemic attitude is no longer aimed toward the object but toward the hearer. When compared, the two figures demonstrate a profile shift from the object to the subject of conceptualization; thus, the diachronic development of *I think* follows the process of subjectification. According to Diessel and Tomasello (2001), interestingly, child language acquisition of the expression *I think* follows the opposite direction of diachronic change: Children first acquire the parenthetical usage of *I think* and subsequently acquire its usage as a matrix clause. This profile shift in an opposite direction is called "objectification" (Verhagen 2007: 73).[2]

Verhagen (2007) argued that the adjustment or negotiation of information between the speaker and the hearer (but not just the construal of the speaker) is strongly reflected in the meaning of some linguistic expressions. Ordinary expressions can be placed between maximally objective and highly subjective ones, and the semantic change and extensions of synchronic usages can be explained by the profile shift: subjectification and objectification.

5.3.6 Current Discourse Space

Verhagen (2007) described both the different perspectives and dynamic processes related to the coordination of information between the two conceptualizers. This is reflected in his description of profiled elements on the ground. These are not profiled in CG, Langacker's framework, unless the conceptualizer is onstage and objectively construed. In contrast, Langacker (2001, 2008) assumed the CDS model in describing the dynamic nature of conceptualizations in conversation. As shown in Figure 5.1 above, CDS describes the flow of conceptualizations and continuously updates itself over time. This is defined as everything shared by the speaker and the hearer at the time of speech, including how they appreciate the ongoing conversation itself.

> ... the current discourse space (CDS), defined as everything presumed to be shared by the speaker and hearer as the basis for discourse at a given moment. ... as discourse proceeds, it is continually updated as each successive utterance processed.
> (Langacker 2008: 281)

> Besides the context of speech, the CDS includes a body of knowledge presumed to be shared and reasonably accessible. It also includes the speaker's and hearer's apprehension of the ongoing discourse itself: ... .
> (Langacker 2001: 145)

CDS is illustrated in Figure 5.11 below. The three rounded rectangles in the center of the diagram represent previous, current, and anticipated discourse (the usage event), respectively, and the discourse flow as a whole. Inside a usage event, which produces an actual utterance, we find "objective content" (which corresponds to the notion of "viewing frame" that will be introduced later), profile, and ground. Ground includes not only the speaker and hearer, but also their interaction, which is depicted by a bidirectional arrow. Although it differs in the degree of its involvement in any expression, the role of the ground is reflected in all speech acts or linguistic expression. Even in statements, interactional action is related in that the speaker directs the hearer's attention to a certain object:

> Though statements are sometimes forcefully made, this is not intrinsic to the scenario. It specifies only the minimal speaker-hearer interaction (double-headed arrow), where the interlocutors apprehend one another and attend to what is said.
> (Langakcer 2008: 473)

CDS also includes "transient context" to apprehend the ongoing discourse, which can be a physical, linguistic, cultural, or social context, and stable knowledge. Mutual understanding in the discourse is achieved only when all these elements are dynamically correlated.

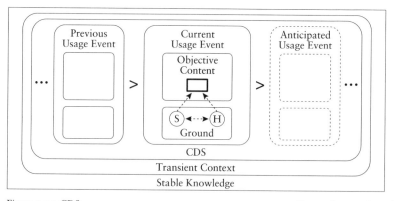

Figure 5.11: CDS　　　　　　　　　　　　　　　　　(Langacker 2008: 466)

Discourse consists of a series of usage events and a usage event can be anything that helps understand the ongoing discourse.

> Conceptually, a usage event includes the expression's full contextual understanding – not only what is said explicitly but also what is inferred, as well as everything evoked as the basis for its apprehension.
> (ibid. 457–458).

A usage event or viewing frame is composed of a phonological pole and a semantic pole that comprise a symbolic assembly. Furthermore, each pole is divided into three "channels," which belong to the viewing frame. A viewing frame includes any kind of thing or concept. It is not the case that only one channel is foregrounded in discourse, but that multiple channels are always co-

CHAPTER 5 A COGNITIVE LINGUISTIC ACCOUNT OF *I MEAN* 63

ordinated in a complex manner.

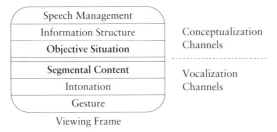

Figure 5.12: Viewing frame (Langacker 2001: 146)

Crucially, however, what appears in this window – the *content* of their coordinated conception – can be anything at all. ... The viewing frame can be directed anywhere. ... Moreover, ... at each pole we can reasonably posit multiple *channels*, which have a certain amount of independence but are nonetheless coordinated in complex ways. (ibid. 145)

The information structure channel includes the notions of old and new information, while speech management entails the notion of turn-taking.

Under information structure, I include such factors as emphasis, discourse topic, and status of information as given versus new. Speech management pertains to such matters as turn taking and holding or relinquishing the floor. (ibid. 145–146)

For example, the CDS and channels describe the filler *uh*, as shown in Figure 5.13.

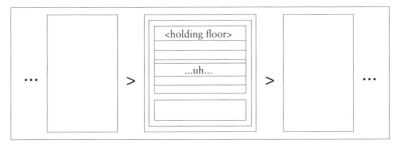

Figure 5.13: *Uh* as a filler (Ibid. 148)

This figure represents the conceptualization of *uh*, which takes place in the Information Structure channel, and the conceptualization and realization of the phonological pole comprising a symbolic structure.

Langacker (2001) inexplicitly indicates that CG, especially the idea of CDS, subsumes the concept of saving face. For instance, the Spanish second-person singular pronoun *tu* shows an intimacy toward the hearer, in contrast to its formal counterpart *usted*. In terms of Politeness Theory, the speaker can be said to select *tu* to save the H's PF, but choose *usted* to save the H's NF. Figure 5.14 represents the cognitive process relative to *tu*.

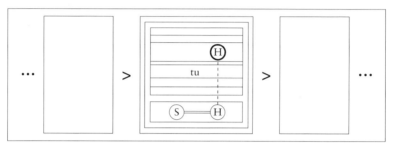

Figure 5.14: Spanish second person pronoun *tu* (Ibid. 148)

As *tu* means *you* in English, the onstage conceptualizer H is profiled in the Objective Situation channel and corresponds to the hearer of the ground (which is depicted by the vertical dotted line. In CG, dotted lines connecting two elements normally represent correspondence and are called "correspondence lines"). The intimacy evoked when using the expression *tu* is illustrated by a double line connecting S and H. In the diagram, intimacy toward the hearer or the consideration for the hearer's PF is represented by interaction of the ground:

> In regard to vocalization, this unit specifies the sequence *tu* as its segmental content. Beyond this, as part of speaker/hearer interaction in the ground, the unit conveys a relationship of familiarity or solidarity (represented diagrammatically by a double line connecting S and H).
>
> (ibid.148–149)

Langacker (2008) suggests three levels of discourse organization: effective level, epistemic level, and discursive level:

> … there is evidence for positing three levels of organization: the **effective** level, pertaining to occurrences; the **epistemic** level, pertaining to

knowledge of occurrences; and an intersubjective **discursive** level, where the relevant occurrences are those of the discourse itself. (ibid. 484)

Through careful observation of Langacker's (2008) examples, the three levels can be paraphrased as follows.

(i) Effective Level: the level relative to an objectively construed occurrence or event
(ii) Epistemic Level: the level relative to the conceptualizer's judgment of the occurrence
(iii) Discursive Level: the level relative to speech acts and inferences

These three levels are realized in the following uses of *because*.

(49) a. The candle went out *because* the oxygen was exhausted. [Effective]
b. He was mad at me *because* I flirted with his wife. [Effective]
c. She must be home, *because* her lights are on. [Epistemic]
d. Are you busy tonight, *because* I've got tickets to the game? [Discursive]

(Sweetser 1990, quoted in Langacker 2008: 484)

In (49a), the connective *because* shows the causal relationship between the extinction of the fire and the exhaustion of oxygen. While the two events are physically related in (49a), they are mentally related in (49b). Nevertheless, because both relationships are at the level of objective content, both uses are invoked at the effective level. In (49c) and (49d), respectively, the fact that someone's lights are on is the reason for the speaker's judgment that this person is at home, and the fact that the speaker has the tickets is the reason why he asks the question. Because these reasons are based on the speaker's judgment and justification of the speech act of asking, the former and latter are positioned at the epistemic level and discursive level, respectively.[3]

In Figure 5.15 and Table 5.1 below, the uses of *because* and the corresponding three levels are illustrated by CDS.

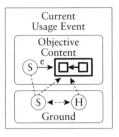

Figure 5.15: Levels of CDS related to *because*

☐◄─☐	Effective Level: Causal relationship between two occurrences (= (49a-b))
(S)─ᵉ→	Epistemic Level: Reason for the judgment of the conceptualizer (= (49c))
(S)◄--►(H)	Discursive Level: Reason for speech act of asking or reinforcement of the speaker's implication (= (49c))

Table 5.1: Levels of CDS related to *because*

5.3.7 Anchoring Structure

Langacker (2009, 2015) proposed an analysis of clausal structure or order of representation that introduces the notion of an "anchor." This section analyzes clause structures based on anchors and anchoring structure. The anchoring structure is semantically or functionally motivated. In other words, specific positions of clause structure bear certain functions, rather than the elements themselves. In short, the anchoring structure represents the functional order of [anchor + core + remainder]. The sequence can be observed at any level of structure: sentence, clause, and "(existential) core" level. The major concern of clauses is the "existence" of the event. That is, the most crucial factor for clauses is whether the event has occurred. Verbal tense takes on the role of demonstrating the existence of the event, and it is called the "existential verb" ($V_{\exists}$). The subject and $V_{\exists}$ comprise the "existential core," ($C_{\exists}$) which forms the simplest structure of the "baseline clause."[4] In addition, the baseline clause, elaborated by modals and perspectival element (perfect, progressive, or passive), comprises the more complicated "basic clause." Although existence is the principal concern of the clause, the element that first appears has a function as important as $V_{\exists}$, namely the "anchor" function. "Anchor" has been defined in relation to similar notions, such as "topic," "frame," "reference point," and "starting point" (Langacker 2009, 2015), but its main function is to enable the speaker to represent and the hearer to understand the propositional content.

A topic (as usually understood) is thus a particular kind of anchor. Being more abstract, the notion "anchor" is even harder to characterize conceptually than is "topic." Impressionistically and metaphorically, an anchor might be described as "framing" the clausal proposition: an instruction to interpret it with respect to a particular domain of knowledge or a certain aspect of the situation described. In a general sense it is also a kind of **reference point** (Langacker 1993), selected for discourse reasons as the initial point of access for representing or apprehending that situation.   (Langakcer 2009: 250)

In a sentence, clause, or core, the anchor is located in the initial position, and serves as a topic for better understanding the propositional content, clause, and schematic process represented by the core. The anchoring structure of (50) is illustrated in Figure 5.16 below.

(50)   Your son, at home he has always been pleasant, hasn't he?
                                                    (Langacker 2015: 31)

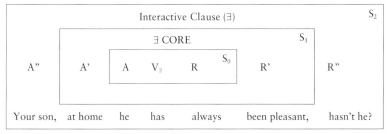

Figure 5.16: Anchoring structure   (Ibid. 31)

Anchors can be divided into a "descriptive anchors" (A) and a "discursive anchors" (A'). The former functions as references to elaborate the schematic process of the core, and its default anchor is the subject. Although the latter also functions as a reference point, it is motivated by the discourse structure. A discursive anchor includes a clause-external anchor (A"), which functions as a topic to aid in understanding of the proposition, and a clause-internal anchor (A'), which functions as a clause-internal topic. In addition, discursive anchors can be further divided into anchors related to existence (which triggers inversion) and anchors that are irrelevant to existence, whereby the latter is related to effective means of presentations, such as *speech management, interclausal connections, information structure, order of presentation, and the packaging of content* (ibid. 20).[5]

Speech management includes such matters as turn taking, holding or yielding the floor, and offstage indications of assent or disagreement. Elements specifying interclausal connections range from having substantial descriptive content (*after*, *because*, *then*) to being purely discursive (*moreover*, *furthermore*, and *so*). Information structure (e.g. notions like topic and informational focus) pertains to the discourse status of entities with respect to their intersubjective availability. (ibid. 20)

5.4 Analysis from Cognitive Linguistics

5.4.1 On Semantic and Pragmatic Functions

5.4.1.1 Subjectification in Verhagen (2005, 2007)

Chapter 3 discussed the motivation for the use of *I mean* in terms of Grice's Conversational Principle, the four maxims, and Politeness Theory. However, these theories lack consistency in their pragmatic accounts.

In this section, the usages of turn-keeping/taking and the usages at what-is-said, implicature, and face levels will all be comprehensively explained as a profile shift in the process of subjectification (Verhagen 2007). More elements of the subject of conceptualization are profiled for these usages, whose original meanings have survived, while more elements of the ground are profiled for more functional usages, whose component meanings have been completely lost.

5.4.1.1.1 Objective Construal Configuration I: Original Meanings

Before further discussion of *I mean* as a discourse marker, we first address the cognitive process underlying the original meanings of *I mean*. Its original meanings can be observed in the following examples:

(51)   a. "Yeah, *I meant* that."
       b. "*I* didn't *mean* to interrupt you."
       c. "And she never returned."
          "What do you mean, she never returned?"
          "*I mean* that she died on her journey." (COCA)

In (51a-c), the speaker clarifies what is represented or conveyed by the previous utterance. Since *I mean* can be paraphrased by *I intended to* ... or *I signified by* ... without changing their utterance meanings, the meanings of the expression's individual components appear to be strongly reflected in these usages. The cognitive process related to the original meanings can be illustrated as shown in

Figure 5.17.

> Object of conceptualization:
> Subject of conceptualization (Ground): 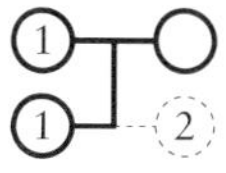
>
> Figure 5.17: Original meanings of *I mean*

In the original usages of *I mean*, the speaker, the process designated by *mean*, and the reference are all objectively construed and profiled. Evidence for these profiles comes from the fact that the verb *mean* can bear tense, as shown in (51a-b), and that the subject can be anybody other than the first-person pronoun in the original usage without affecting the meaning of the verb *mean*, as in *She didn't mean to interrupt you*, but not as a discourse marker.

Although Figures 5.17 and 5.9 look the same, this does not imply that the cognitive processes of *I think* and *I mean* are the same. In fact, they are considerably different: The epistemic stance toward the propositional content is profiled in the former expression, while the latter highlights the relationship between the two propositional contents or actions, rather than the construal.[6]

5.4.1.1.2 Objective Construal Configuration II: The What-Is-Said Level

In the original usages of *I mean*, the meaning of the verb *mean*, equivalent to *to signify* and *to intend*, is strongly reflected in the expression, and the speaker is objectively construed. The original meanings are also reflected in the usages of *I mean* at the what-is-said level, although their cognitive process differs from the original usages.

(52) JA: Do Isabella and Connor come down to Nashville a lot?
      NK: No, they don't. They're not crazy about Nashville. They're so grown up now. *I mean*, they're adults.   (= (24))

In (52), as mentioned above, the speaker does not obey Grice's Maxims of Manner in the preceding utterance, but obeys it after *I mean*, when the speaker replaces the phrase *grown up* with *adults*. In other words, by using *I mean*, she shows the relationship between the propositional contents before and after *I mean*.

The following example is also cited from Chapter 4 and belongs at the what-is-said level.

(53) 01 J: Where in Florida are you from?
      02 N: I am from Melbourne, Florida. Have you been to Florida

03		before?
04	J:	I haven't been to Florida. ***I mean*** I have. I've been to
05		Orlando. (= (22))

In (53), the speaker violates the Maxim of Quality before *I mean* and follows it in the subsequent discourse. As in (52), the speaker uses *I mean* to replace the information before and after *I mean*. Therefore, once again, the speaker uses *I mean* to connect the propositional contents.

Although *I mean* relates to the propositional contents in both (52) and (53), the former connects similar information, while the latter connects contradictory information. This seems to indicate that *I mean* at the what-is-said level varies in the degree of reflection of its original meaning, and that a gradation exists in the usages of *I mean* from the matrix clause to the discourse marker. Obviously, *I mean* reflects its components' meanings and functions more like matrix clause when it relates similar propositions, but loses much of its original meaning and functions more like discourse marker when connecting contradictory information. Because this usage of *I mean* refers more to the relationships in propositional content, the speaker is no longer objectively construed and only the relation between the previous and following utterances is focused. The construal configuration for this usage can be illustrated as shown in Figure 5.18.

Object of conceptualization:
Subject of conceptualization (Ground):

Figure 5.18: *I mean* at the what-is-said level

As in the original usages, the speaker of the ground and the construal are profiled. This is because in both usages, the speaker refers to an element at the level of the object of conceptualization: propositional content, speaker's intention, or the relationship between two propositional contents. In the usage discussed in this section, the speaker and his reference to the object are not objectively construed (or no longer focused); instead, the relationship between the previous and following utterances acquires more cognitive salience.[7]

5.4.1.1.3 Subjective Construal Configuration I: The Implicature Level
Whereas *I mean* at the what-is-said level reflects the original meaning of *to signify* as in (51c), *I mean* at the implicature level reflects the alternative meaning of *to intend* as seen in (51b).

(54) a. He says, "Oh, I wish you could come with me!"
b. And I said—I was very pro- proper and prim!
c. And I said, "Oh, I couldn't go away with you."
d. And he says, "*I mean* let's get married!"
e. And I said, "Oh, okay!" (= (3))

As mentioned above, the speaker *He* in (54) intended a proposal of marriage in line (a), although the hearer did not interpret it in that way (line (c)). Thus, the speaker made it explicit by verbalizing his intention in line (d). Before his use of *I mean*, the speaker flouted the Maxim of Quantity by implying that moving in together would be merely one reason for marriage. Because of this, the hearer instead interpreted his intended marriage proposal literally. This use can be classified at the implicature level because the implicature that the speaker wanted to convey (which has been generated by flouting the Maxim of Quantity) in turn violates the Maxim of Quality. Thus, the speaker signaled the violation of the Maxim of Quality by using *I mean*. If the speaker had only flouted the Maxim of Quantity, he would not have used *I mean*. He used it to show that it was not his intended implicature; in other words, he did not obey the Maxim of Quality at the implicature level.

In the discussion on the modification of speaker intention by *I mean*, Schiffrin (1987: 296) noted that the speaker doubts whether his intention is successfully conveyed to the hearer. In (54), from the utterance in line (c), it is obvious that the speaker *he* of line (d) knew that the hearer did not interpret his intention correctly. However, the point is not whether the speaker became aware of the fact that his intention was missed by the hearer beforehand. More importantly, the speaker's use of *I mean* was possibly triggered only by the assumption of misunderstanding. In fact, there is no outright clue at all in the following example.

(55) A: Have you guys been to Australia before?
B: He has. *I mean*, I'm going to visit there next year though.
(Excerpt from (26))

In (55), the speaker B uses *I mean* to show that the implicature generated by the preceding discourse (by flouting the Maxim of Quantity) is not what he intended to express. Therefore, *I mean* here signals a violation of the Maxim of Quality at the implicature level. Although examples (54) and (55) differ in their presence of obvious clues about the hearer's misunderstanding, they share the same contradiction between the speaker's anticipation of what the hearer thinks and what the speaker wants to convey to the hearer, as well as the same attempt to resolve that contradiction. In (54), the contradiction is between the speaker's intention to propose marriage and the hearer's literal understanding of his words, whereas in (55), the contradiction is between the speaker's implicature of not having been to Australia and his plan to go there in the near future. In both cases, the speaker uses *I mean* to solve the contradiction, by making the intention explicit in the former case and by adding information about the speaker himself in the latter.

Verhagen (2007) referred to the notion of "mental space" (MS) originally from Fauconnier (1994), and calls the coordination of information in between the speaker's MS and hearer's MS "intersubjectivity." The coordination of information in (54) and (55) is exactly what he calls an intersubjective coordination: The speaker states his intention explicitly (to follow Grice's maxim), assuming it has been misconveyed to the hearer. The construal configuration for the usage of implicature level is depicted in Figure 5.19.

Object of conceptualization:
Subject of conceptualization (Ground):

Figure 5.19: *I mean* at the implicature level

The intersubjective coordination is illustrated by the profile of the horizontal line connecting the elements of the ground. The vertical line is also profiled because the speaker replaces or clarifies information for the sake of the hearer and so the speaker attempts to address the hearer's attention to the same entity.[8]

5.4.1.1.4 Subjective Construal Configuration II: The Face Level
In addition to correcting violations of Grice's Maxims, saving face can also be a motivation for using *I mean*.

(56) The CO's smile was really very pleasant.
"It's what you joined to do, isn't it?"
"No, sir. *I mean* Yes, sir. I mean, I'm an actor, sir"
He gulped and went rushing on. "I have to start rehearsal on
Monday, I've got a new job to go back to."   (Excerpt from (38))

In (56), the soldier is an actor in the army, as he explains in the last part of his utterance, and he does not want to fight on the front lines. Therefore, the utterance *No, sir* before *I mean* is his honest answer to the officer's question. However, his honest answer is not what the hearer expected, and it can be considered inappropriate and disrespectful, especially in light of the relationship between a soldier and his commanding officer (CO). To redress the threat to the H's NF, the speaker uses *I mean* and changes the utterance to the expected, appropriate, and respectful *Yes, sir*.

No coordination of the relationship between the different kinds of information can be observed in the process of saving hearer's face. Because Verhagen (2005, 2007) did not mention saving face, here we assume the notion of face-saving to be an element of intersubjective coordination. By placing "threatening the hearer's NF" in the hearer's MS and "redressing the threatened face" in the speaker's MS, the adjustment of face work can be explained in a similar fashion to the coordination of specific information. The construal configuration of this usage is also illustrated as in Figure 5.19, where the adjustment of face is represented by the profile of the entire ground, and the joint attention to the preceding utterance (which actually motivated the speaker to use *I mean*; therefore, it is assumed to have high cognitive salience in Verhagen's sense), which is demonstrated by the profile of the vertical line.

5.4.1.1.5 Subjective Construal Configuration III: The Face and Speech Management Levels

Fox Tree and Schrock (2002: 733–734) noted that *I mean* relates to positive politeness, in that it reminds the hearer of casual talk, and to negative politeness, in that it weakens the speaker's commitment to the statement. If the speaker intentionally uses *I mean* to create a casual atmosphere, uttering *I mean* itself functions to save the hearer's face. However, we approach this with some skepticism, because few examples seem to represent the speaker's obvious intention to create a casual atmosphere. On the other hand, some examples of the latter's function, relative to negative politeness, can be observed in our data.

(57) 01 A: No. No. Tuition is 40,000 now.
      02 B: Really? It went up?
      03 A: It's 40,000.
      04 C: Forty thousand?
      05 B: It's like the average person's annual salary.
      06 C: Yeah.
      07 A: Yeah.
      08 C: Do you think it's worth it?
      09 A: *I mean*, I love Tufts but yeah, it's not the greatest like I
      10   don't even see where all the money is being spent and I
      11   don't really know.   (CRMTP 19)

In (57), participants talk about university tuition, and their belief is that it is expensive. After the question posed by C, speaker A expresses her opinion about tuition and the school in general. The *I mean* in line 09 is not used to take a turn of the conversation, as it is used after the question (at so-called Transition Relevance Place [TRP]) (cf. Sacks, Schegloff, and Jefferson 1974: 716), nor is it used to replace information from the preceding utterance *Yeah* from line 07. In this case, it is more reasonable to assume that *I mean* is used to weaken the speaker's responsibility for the subsequent utterance *I love Tufts*. In fact, a negative statement follows that statement. In the CRMTP data, five of the eight examples contained a negative statement that followed after *but*, as seen in (57).

When *I mean* functions by itself to save face, there is no violation of Grice's Maxims, nor is there a threat to the hearer's face in the preceding utterance. Although there appears to be a mismatch between this usage and the definition of *I mean* described in Chapter 1 and developed in Chapter 3, it can be explained as a functional usage that has lost its specific meaning, leaving only a schematic meaning. Again, in terms of pragmatic theory, *I mean* was defined as a marker that shows the speaker's violation of Grice's Maxims or face threat and the speaker's will to obey the maxim or save the face. Therefore, this usage can be explained as a functional *I mean* that has lost the first half of its specific meaning and maintained only the speaker's will to save H's NF.

Usages for turn-holding/taking also do not require a preceding utterance, but they strongly expect a following utterance. As seen in the definition of *I mean* (or discourse makers in general) in previous studies, such as "upcoming modification" (Schiffrin 1987: 296), "forewarning speaker adjustments" (Fox Tree and Schrock 2002: 744), and "parts of speech possessing a power of projection" (Imo 2005: 9), the use of *I mean* always makes the hearer expect a relevant utterance will follow.[9] The following example shows *I mean* for turn-taking.

(58) 01 A: The irony of that though, is I don't think GOP would support us much if you are Latino. Hhh
02 B: Ah, hhh (0.5) tricky. [Unclear]=
03 C: = *I mean*, at one point, didn't he say that his strate, well I
04 don't know if he said it but, it seems like his strategy was
05 just gonna be try not to do anything, because everything he
06 did just made things, made them look worse, so::

(Kobayashi 2013: 162)

In (58), the interlocutors talk about the presidential election of 2009 in the United States. In this conversation, A and B tend to keep their turns and C rarely takes a turn from them. In fact, C simply makes a sound as response to their conversation twice, at around 18 seconds and 30 seconds before line 03. Because there was no relevant preceding utterance, we can conclude that *I mean* in (58) is uttered to deprive a turn in the conversation from those interested in politics. The usage of *I mean* signals that relevant information will follow, which corresponds to the latter half of the first definition of *I mean*. The usage of turn-keeping/taking can also be accounted for as a functional use that has lost its specific meaning and maintained only the speaker's will to continue the utterance after *I mean*.

I mean to save face and hold/take a turn of conversation are both schematized usages. They can be illustrated as shown in Figure 5.20.

Object of conceptualization:
Subject of conceptualization (Ground):

Figure 5.20: *I mean* at the face level and speech management levels

Because the speaker uses *I mean* without a relevant preceding utterance, the vertical line that shows the joint attention toward the object of conceptualization is not profiled. Only the elements of the ground are profiled because the speaker adjusts the face work or turn work in consideration of the hearer by using *I mean*. Verhagen (2007) defines expressions of greetings, such as *Hi!*, and apologies, such as *Sorry*, as highly subjective expressions and illustrates the cognitive process related to these expressions as Figure 5.20. The commonality between these expressions mentioned in Verhagen (2007) and the use of *I mean* to save face by itself or to hold/take a turn is a form of intersubjective coordination without the exchange of specific information, but with more social and cultural based interactions. Therefore, these expressions belong at neither the what-is-said level nor at the implicature level, but at a more social level.

5.4.1.1.6 Usages of *I mean* and Subjectification

As mentioned above, Verhagen (2007) defines the shift in profile from more profiled elements of the object of conceptualization to more profiled elements of the ground as "subjectification." By comparing construal configurations of examples from (51) to (58), the relation between the usages of *I mean* can be explained as a process of subjectification.

Object of conceptualization:
Subject of conceptualization (Ground):

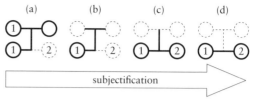

subjectification

- (a) corresponds to (51) (original meanings)
  (51b) *I* didn't *mean* to interrupt you.
- (b) is for (52) and (53) (what-is-said level)
  (52) They're so grown up now. *I mean*, they're adults.
  (53) I haven't been to Florida. *I mean*, I have.
- (c) is for (54) trough (56) (implicature Level)
  (54) "Oh, I wish you could come with me!"
  "I mean, let's get married!"
  (55) He has. *I mean*, I'm going to visit there next year though.
  (56) "No, sir. *I mean*, Yes, sir."
- (d) is for (57) and (58) (face level and turn level)
  (57) *I mean*, I love Tufts but yeah, ...
  (58) *I mean*, at one point, didn't he say that his strate, ...?

Figure 5.21: The usages of *I mean* as a process of subjectification

The construal configuration in Figure 5.21(a) represents the two original usages in (51). Because the speaker and his reference to the propositional content are objectively construed, all elements of the object of conceptualization are profiled. In 5.21(b), which shows *I mean* in (52) and (53), the horizontal line of the object of conceptualization is profiled contrastively because the subject *I* is no longer construed objectively and only the connection between the two propositional elements becomes salient at this level. Configuration (c) represents *I mean* at the implicature level in examples (54), (55), and (56), in which the joint attention and intersubjective coordination of specific information or face are profiled. The former is profiled because the motivations for using *I mean*, namely implicature and threatening of face, originate from the preceding utterance. The highly subjective configuration (d) shows the usage of *I mean* that functions by itself to save face in (57) and turn-taking in (58). They involve a schematic (or more social) intersubjective coordination, such as adjustments of face and turn. The usages of *I mean* can be ordered in terms of the cognitive salience as part of different cognitive processes.

5.4.1.2 Problems with the Analysis in Terms of Intersubjectivity (Verhagen 2005, 2007)

Because of intersubjectivity (Verhagen 2005, 2007), the interpersonal usages of *I mean* that have been labeled "modification of speaker attitude," "causal meaning," "monitoring," and "interpersonal" in previous studies comprehensively reanalyzed, in terms of intersubjective coordination and interrelations in the process of subjectification. Though it helps to compare less-intersubjective usages with more-intersubjective ones, it is still unclear how the intersubjective usages relate to each other. In the next section, interaction, a portion of grounding connecting the two conceptualizers, will be discussed further from the perspective of the CDS. This theoretical framework in CG leads to clear distinction of the unaccounted usages through description of their cognitive processes.

5.4.1.3 *I mean* at Different Levels of CDS

Langacker's (2001, 2008) CDS provides relevant notions for finer-grained description of the "interaction" part of the ground. CDS encompasses various linguistic phenomena: propositional content, epistemic attitudes, speech acts, implicatures, turn-holding/taking, and even politeness (cf. Kobayashi 2016). In short, the intersubjective usages belong to different discourse levels in CDS: the discursive level, face level, and speech management level. These usages will be organized according to how the speaker and hearer construe the situation.

5.4.1.3.1 The Effective Level

The what-is-said level roughly corresponds to the effective level in that the speaker connects two entities from the propositional content either by *I mean*, as shown in (59) and (60) or *because*, as seen below (61a-b).

(59) JA: Do Isabella and Connor come down to Nashville a lot?
NK: No, they don't. They're not crazy about Nashville. They're so grown up now. *I mean*, they're adults. (= (25))
(60) I haven't been to Florida. *I mean*, I have. (Excerpt from (23))
(61) a. The candle went out *because* the oxygen was exhausted.
b. He was mad at me *because* I flirted with his wife. (= (49a-b))

They differ in the degree of how specifically the speaker construes the relationship. As previously noted, speakers use *I mean* because they are violating the Maxim of Quality (or Manner) at the level of what is said. The relationship before and after *I mean*, as seen in (59) and (60), can be paraphrased as *adults rather than grown ups* and *I have been to Florida not I haven't been there*. In addition, there should be more candidates for what-is-said level paraphrases, such as *in addition to* and *because*. On the other hand, the connective *because* (as shown in (61a-b)) and adverb *therefore* profile causal and ordinal relationships, respectively (cf. Langacker 2001: 149, 2008: 484–485). Hence, the relationship between propositional content profiled in case of *I mean* is more schematic than that of other connectives and adverbs, such as *because* and *therefore*.

The cognitive process related to *I mean* at the what-is-said level is depicted in Figure 5.22. At the effective level, the speaker uses *I mean* to indicate that the propositional content expressed before *I mean* is not what he or she wanted to convey, and *I mean* itself connects the two propositions. In the diagram, the two propositions expressed in the previous and anticipated usage events (P_1 and P_2), and their relationship are profiled.

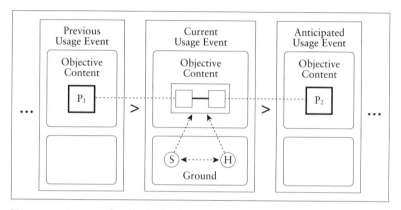

Figure 5.22: *I mean* at the effective level

5.4.1.3.2 The Discursive Level

Speech acts and implicatures that are relevant at the discursive level are those that account for the usages of *I mean* at the implicature level.

(62) "Oh, I wish you could come with me." ... "*I mean*, let's get married."

(Excerpt from (3))

(63) Are you busy tonight, *because* I've got tickets to the game? (= (49d))

In (62), the speaker makes his intention from the preceding utterance clear to the hearer. *I mean* in (62) has the same function of clarifying the speaker's intention as *because* in (63). As has been frequently mentioned in this book, the clarification achieved by *I mean* is based on the speaker's doubt about the hearer's misunderstanding, whereas the one achieved by *because* is derived from the speaker's hope to strengthen his intention. The cognitive process related to *I mean* at the implicature level is illustrated in Figure 5.23:

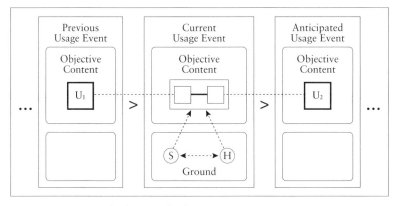

Figure 5.23: *I mean* at the discursive level

At this level, the speaker uses *I mean* because he finds that the hearer has inferred or may infer something the speaker does not intend to convey. The major purpose of using *I mean* is not to correct or add to propositional content in the previous discourse but to resolve the difference between what the speaker and hearer have in mind. In the cognitive process relative to *I mean* at the discursive level, the relationship between what is said in the previous and anticipated usage events is no longer cognitively salient. Therefore, P_1 and P_2 are replaced with U_1 and U_2, where U stands for utterance. The hearer's misunderstanding occurs at the level of the ground, namely the discursive level in the speaker's mind.

Once again, the relationship at the discursive level should not be more cognitively salient than that at the effective level. This is a matter of degree; effective, discursive, and face levels are ordered as they are with respect to how the relationship is cognitively salient (salient to not salient) and how the interaction of the ground functions (less to more functioning).

5.4.1.3.3 The Face Level

Although Verhagen's (2007) notion of intersubjectivity does not entirely cover the phenomena known as face work and turn work, the notions relevant to CDS can account for the differences between the interpersonal usages of *I mean*. The notions are the interaction between the speaker and hearer, the levels of discourse, and the channels of the viewing frame.

In the following example, the speaker uses *I mean* to show the threat to the H's NF and his will to redress the threat:

(64) "Hi, Damian!" … "I — *I mean* Mr. Flint" (Excerpt from (40))

The cognitive process related to *I mean* at the Face Level can be illustrated by CDS as follows.

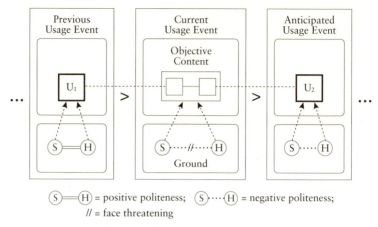

Figure 5.24: *I mean* at the face level

In (64), the speaker attempts to save the H's PF, but he realizes that the H's PF is threatened by his attempt. Subsequently, in the following utterance, he redresses that threat. The speaker's attempt to save the H's PF is illustrated by the double lines of the ground in the previous usage event and the speaker's awareness of the attempt that threatens the H's NF is illustrated by double slashes of the ground (//) in the current usage event. In the space of the anticipated usage event, the redress of the threat is represented by dotted line. The face work related to *I mean* in (64) is represented by the ground in each space. Since the motivation for using *I mean* is in this face work, the relationship between the pieces of propositional content are not cognitively salient, so are no longer profiled.

5.4.1.3.4 The Speech Management Level

There is no need for an argument about the level to which the usage of turn-taking and turn-holding should belong, other than at the speech management level. *I mean* used for turn-keeping will be different from the filler *uh* because the former has the power to create an expectation of a following utterance:

> *I mean* always opens a pragmatic projection, signalling to the recipients that there is something to follow. (Imo 2005: 15)

Therefore, although it is not profiled or foregrounded, the relationship profiled at the effective level is placed slightly for this usage (see §5.4.1.1.5 for more details) and is illustrated by dotted squares, as shown in Figure 5.25.

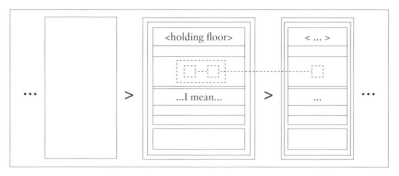

Figure 5.25: *I mean* at the speech management level

5.4.1.3.5 The Usage of *I mean* outside the Scope of CDS

The discourse marker *I mean* has been analyzed through CDS, and the relationships among its various usages were found to be motivated in a theoretically consistent manner. The levels of CDS and related cognitive processes account for the differences between usages. However, CDS, which is a cognitive model meant to describe dynamic conceptualization in discourse, is not sufficiently precise to fully describe all the usages of *I mean*. Once again, we re-examine the example from Schiffrin (1987):

(65) a. He says, "Oh, I wish you could come with me!"
      b. And I said—I was very pro- proper and prim!
      c. And I said, "Oh, I couldn't go away with you."
      d. And he says, "*I mean* let's get married!
      e. And I said, "Oh, okay!"   (= (3))

Example (65) shows at least three steps in the speaker's use of *I mean* (in line (d)): $_{1)}$ the speaker intends to propose marriage with his utterance *I wish you could come with me* (in line (a)), $_{2)}$ he realizes that the hearer interprets his previous utterance literally, and $_{3)}$ he realizes that the hearer thinks that the speaker means it literally, too. Therefore, $_{4)}$ he makes his intention clear to the hearer. This complex process of conceptualization might be explained by Verhagen's notion of intersubjectivity with the help of Fauconnier's (1994) MS, but descriptions by CDS cover more phenomena, because the latter seeks an explanation of the process based on the interaction between the speaker and the hearer. Langacker (2008) indicated that interaction possibly includes the notions of intersubjective coordination of information and joint attention, which is similar to Verhagen's notion, although he does not further discuss this matter:

> A key factor in its (an expression's) meaning is the interaction of the speaker and hearer, each engaged in assessing what the other knows, intends, and is currently attending to. (ibid. 465)

An observation of Figures 5.22 through 5.25 seems to suggest that one conceptualization relates to one linguistic element (or one intonation unit [IU]) in CDS. In other words, each discourse space in CDS includes one conceptualization that corresponds to one element (or IU), given Langacker's (2001, 2008) descriptions. For this reason, we insist that the existing model of CDS cannot account for the complex process related to *I mean* mentioned above. In the next section, an updated version of CDS will be introduced to describe this dynamic cognitive process, in which one conceptualization contains multiple phases.

5.4.1.3.6 A New Model of CDS with Multiple Phases

According to Langacker (2001, 2008), CDS consists of a symbolic structure in which one form (phonological realization) pairs with one meaning (conceptualization). It means that the multiplex process related to *I mean* cannot be illustrated by CDS. The process in example (65) can be described as follows.

1) The speaker intends to propose marriage with his utterance *I wish you could come with me*.
2) The speaker realizes that the hearer interprets his previous utterance literally.
3) The speaker knows the hearer finds that the speaker also means the preceding utterance literally.
4) The speaker makes his intention clear to the hearer.

A new version of CDS including these steps is illustrated in Figure 5.26 (cf. Langacker 2008: 474; Yamanashi 2001: 187), which contains multiple phases for one conceptualization.

CHAPTER 5 A COGNITIVE LINGUISTIC ACCOUNT OF *I MEAN* 83

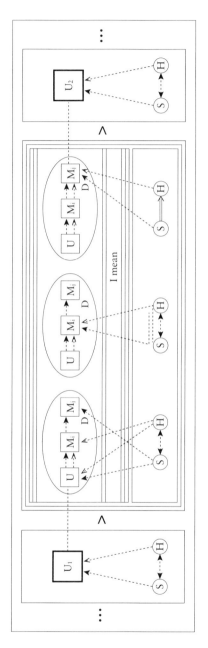

U = utterance; D = dominion; ‒‒‒▶ = mental path of S; ‒‒‒▶ = mental path of H; ▼‒‒▶ = interaction;
⇒ = social and psychological force; ‒‒‒‒ = correspondence line;
U₁ = previous utterance (e.g., *I wish you could come with me.*);
U₂ = following utterance (e.g., *Let's get married.*);
M₁ = literal meaning of U₁; Mᵢ = intended/implicated meaning of M₁

Figure 5.26: A new CDS: *I mean* at the discursive level

The process illustrated in Figure 5.26 can be described as follows.

> < The cognitive process related to *I mean* at the discursive level >
> Phase 1: S and H direct their attentions to different entities (S→U→M_i→M_j = S→M_j; H→U→M_i = H→M_i)
> Phase 2: S finds that H is attending to an entity different from S's and that H thinks S also attends to the same entity as H (S→H→M_j; (S→)H→S→M_j)
> Phase 3: S utters *I mean* (and the following utterance) to let H know that they are directing their attention to different entities and S attempts to draw H's attention to the same entity (S→H, S→M_j, H→M_j)

According to Brinton (2008), the use of *I mean* is motivated by the speaker's doubt that his intention was conveyed to the hearer. However, she only mentions this in a note without further comment. Phase 2 above is provided as theoretical background in addition to her comment. The point of using *I mean* is not only to show the speaker knows the hearer's misunderstanding but also to show the speaker knows that the hearer thinks his or her idea is the same as the speaker's.

Itkonen (2008) quoted Lewis (1969), in defining common knowledge; X can be an object of the common knowledge, if and only if the conditions shown below are true between the speaker and hearer:

(66) a. A knows – 1 X
      b. A knows – 2 that B knows – 1 X
      c. A knows – 3 that B knows – 2 that A knows – 1 X   (Itkonen 2008: 288)

Three-level knowledge of this kind necessarily occurs in all institutional encounters, according to Itkonen (2008), although this does not mean that this kind of knowledge works perfectly in actual conversations. In the process of generating common knowledge, *I mean* refers to both the speaker and hearer's information at specific levels of knowledge. The cognitive process relative to *I mean* at the effective level includes knowledge of (66a), in that the speaker (= A) replaces the propositional content (= X) by *I mean*. At the discursive level, *I mean* includes (66b-c) because the speaker knows the hearer's (= B) misunderstanding (= 66b) and also knows that the hearer thinks that the speaker thinks the same way (= 66c). At the final stage of Phase 2, the speaker utters *I mean* in an attempt to direct the hearer's attention to the same entity. After *I mean* is uttered in the anticipated usage event, joint attention between the speaker and hearer is achieved.

Also for *I mean* at the face level, multiple phases seem to be necessary in the description of its cognitive process.

(67) "It's what you joined to do, isn't it?" "No, sir. ***I mean*** Yes, sir. I mean, I'm an actor, sir." (Excerpt from (38))

In (67), the speaker threatens the hearer's NF with the utterance of his honest opinion *No, sir*, so he saves the face by replacing it with an answer that is favorable to the hearer. The steps related to *I mean* in (67) can be described as follows:

1) The speaker saves the hearer's face in the preceding utterance.
2) The speaker realizes that he had threatened the hearer's face in the preceding utterance.
3) The speaker redresses the threat.

The cognitive process related to *I mean* in (67) can be illustrated in Figure 5.27.

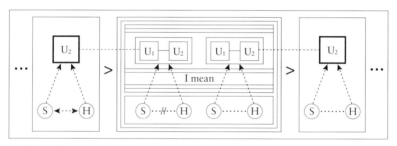

Figure 5.27: A new CDS: *I mean* at the face level

In the previous discourse space, a politeness relationship is not involved in the interaction of the ground. This is because the speaker gave his honest opinion before *I mean* and hence face-saving was not involved. The subsequent steps are described below:

< The cognitive process related to *I mean* at the face level >
 Phase 1: S finds that H knows of the threat to the hearer's face
 Phase 2: S shows his will to redress the threat to the hearer's face

This section suggests a new version of CDS consisting of multiple phases. For precise descriptions of the cognitive processes related to *I mean* at the implicature level and face level, at least two to three phases are required. The major problem with the existing CDS is that the existing framework aims to describe only the result phase of the event in which both conceptualizers jointly attend to the same entity, and little consideration is given to the cases in which they direct their attentions to different objects. Nevertheless, only by adding Phase 2 at the implicature level and Phase 1 at the face level does the description of the cognitive process related to *I mean* reflect its dynamic nature accurately. Moreover, the lively and dynamically developing functions of interactions are better described as a cognitive process with multiple phases.

5.4.2 Relationships between the Usages of *I mean*

In this chapter, the usages of *I mean* are classified according to their related cognitive processes in terms of levels of organization (of discourse) and channels (Langacker 2001, 2008). I suggested that the classification of *I mean* includes four levels: the effective, discursive, speech management, and face levels. At the effective level, the relationship between the elements of propositional content is profiled, while this relationship is backgrounded at the subsequent levels. Instead, mental and social relationships are foregrounded. The mental path from the source meaning to the target meaning and the joint attention of the speaker and hearer are activated at the discursive level, whereas the speaker and hearer attend to the more abstract notion of turn-taking at the speech management level, and social interaction is the main function at the face level. Figure 5.28 below illustrates how the levels are cognitively organized and motivated.

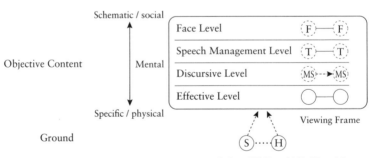

Figure 5.28: The relationships between the usages of *I mean*

In the viewing frame, more specific and physical levels lead to more profiling of objective content and fewer interaction functions. In contrast, the more schematic and social levels lead to less profiling of objective content and more interaction functions. Nevertheless, in all usages, intersubjective relationships (i.e., interactions) are somehow involved even to a minimal degree. *I mean* is not used to build truth-conditional meanings but to create a common understanding between the speaker and the hearer. The definition of *I mean* as "intersubjective adjustment" is based on this fact.

For clarification of the speaker's motivation for using *I mean*, which is the purpose of this study, and for the convenience of description, one token of *I mean* is classified as one level of discourse. However, multiple factors appear to serve as motivation for using it in number of cases. For example, as shown above, *I mean* in the following example is appointed to the effective level (or the what-is-said level) because speaker L does not obey Grice's Maxim of Quantity at the what-is-said level:

(68) 01 M: So...but you speak Japanese, right?
      02 L: Somewhat. *I mean*, I'm like, I can do conversation – I'm
      03   conversationally fluent but like you know there's all those
      04   like levels of speech. My mom is like it's better it you don't.
      05   Don't try.   (= (6))

The speaker explains what her utterance *Somewhat* means in the subsequent utterance and adds information in the utterance following that one. Thus, *I mean* connects the elements of propositional content and shows their relationship. Although it cannot be observed from the typed texts, the vowel "ea" in *I mean* in (68) is longer than others, and seems to serve to maintain a particular turn during the conversation.[10] As Langacker (2001: 145) notes, it is not the case that only one channel is always foregrounded, but that multiple channels are coordinated in a complex manner. Therefore, for one use of *I mean*, multiple channels and levels of representations are involved, and among them, we describe the phenomena as having high and specific cognitive salience depending on the motivation for using *I mean*.

5.4.3 On Positions in Discourse

This section attempts to explain the position of *I mean* in discourse from the perspective of cognitive linguistics. Previous studies mainly focused on its pragmatic functions, not on its syntax nor its position in discourse. These include the high frequency of clause-initial positions (cf. Brinton 2008) and the limitation of clause-internal positions to the usage of correcting (cf. Tanaka and Ishizaki 1994).[11]

I mean appears overwhelmingly in clause-initial position. ... When it is used in the middle of the clause, the entire clause does not take shape as a construction. Thus clause-internal *I mean* tends to be used for correcting the previous utterance.

(Tanaka and Ishizaki 1994: 15, originally in Japanese)

While studies generally agree that *I mean* occurs initially and medially, but rarely in final position the PDE corpora show that parenthetical *I mean* occurs overwhelmingly in initial position, ... (Brinton 2008: 118)

Tanaka and Ishizaki (1994) and Brinton (2008) investigate the characteristics of the positions in discourse from the data of synchronic corpora, but they do not explain why clause-initial *I mean* dominates the data and why the clause-internal *I mean* is limited to usages of correcting. This section proposes that the position of *I mean* is motivated by discourse functions by means of the anchoring structure suggested by Langacker (2009, 2015).

5.4.3.1 *I mean* as a Part of the Core: Original Meanings

As Schiffrin (1987: 296) revealed, the pragmatic meanings of *I mean* are derived from the two original meanings of the verb *mean*: *to signify* and *to intend* as shown in (69a-b) below.

(69) a. "Yeah, *I meant* that."
 b. "*I* didn't *mean* to interrupt you."
 c. "And she never returned."
 "What do you mean, she never returned?"
 "*I mean* that she died on her journey." (= (51))

The verb *mean* bears tense and polarity in (69a-b), so *I meant it* and *I didn't mean* consist of part of the existential core (because the existence of the events is the main concern of clauses). Therefore, *I mean* as a matrix clause could function as a descriptive anchor, and *mean* functions as a remainder of the existential verb or the core. The anchoring structures related to (69a-b) are illustrated in Figures 5.29 and 5.30 respectively.

$C_{\exists}$		R'
A	$V_{\exists}$	
I	*meant*	that.

Figure 5.29: Original meaning of *I mean* (i)

	C₃	R'
A	V₃	
I	didn't	*mean* to interrupt you.

Figure 5.30: Original meaning of *I mean* (ii)

The relationship between the matrix clause and the complement clause, shown in (69c), can be described as the relationship between the basic clause and elaborated clause. The latter functions as a basic grounding and the former as interactive grounding that elaborates upon the polarity and illocutionary force that prompts the conceptualizer to correspond with the actual speaker (cf. Langacker 2009: 235). The complementizer *that* can be considered reference point leading to a proposition and therefore a clause-external anchor. The anchoring structure of the relationship between the matrix clause and the subsequent *that* clause can be illustrated as shown in Figure 5.31; the former functions as an anchor, and the latter functions as an anchored structure.

	C₃		R'		
A	V₃	A'	C₃		R'
			A	V₃	
I	*mean*	that	she	died	on her journey.

Figure 5.31: Original meaning of *I mean* (iii)

I mean as a matrix clause functions as part of the existential core; therefore, it represents the existence of the event.

5.4.3.2 *I mean* as a Discursive Anchor: The Effective and Discursive Levels

The following two examples are classified at the effective level and the discursive level.

(70) 01 J: Where in Florida are you from?
 02 N: I am from Melbourne, Florida. Have you been to Florida
 03 before?
 04 J: I haven't been to Florida. *I mean* I have. I've been to
 05 Orlando. (= (23))
(71) Do you like steak? *I mean*, there is this place called Capital Grill.
(CRMTP 2)

In (70) and (71), the speaker uses *I mean* to clarify the information of the propositional content and his intention, respectively. These usages of *I mean* function as clause-external anchors and provide a topic or frame for better understanding the subsequent proposition. What is provided for *I mean* is a frame "what the speaker truly wants to direct hearer's attention to is going to follow." Figures 5.32 and 5.33 represent the anchoring structures for (70) and (71).

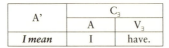

A'	C_3	
	A	V_3
I mean	I	have.

Figure 5.32: *I mean* at the effective level

A'	C_3		R'
	A	V_3	
I mean	there	is	this place called capital grill.

Figure 5.33: *I mean* at the discursive level

At the effective level and discursive level, *I mean* functions as a clause-external anchor, unlike the anchoring structure of the original meanings, where *I* and *mean* have different functions. First, the former *I mean* does not bear tense and therefore cannot form the core (e.g.,² *I haven't been to Florida. I meant I have*). Second, *I mean* cannot correspond with tags. In example (72a), the tag corresponds to the clause that follows *I mean,* while the tag corresponds to *I mean* as a matrix clause in (72b). Because tags schematically represent the core (Langacker 2009: 247), the failure to establish a correspondence with tags indicates that *I mean* no longer functions as part of the core, but rather as an unanalyzable whole.

(72) a. **I mean**, they get paid for serving you, don't they?
b. **She meant** she was frightened, didn't she? (BNC)

5.4.3.3 *I mean* as a Discursive Anchor: The Speech Management Level

Functions such as taking or holding a turn are considered primarily discursive; thus, they are directly motivated by the discourse structure:

> Discursive structures have little content of their own, consisting instead in ways of organizing and presenting descriptive content for interactive purposes as a discourse unfolds. (Langacker 2015: 21)

I mean used for turn-taking functions as a discursive anchor because it initiates the speaker's turn in the conversation and helps the hearer understand that what the speaker truly wants him to pay attention to will follow. It does not matter whether *I mean* appears in the TRP or in the middle of the hearer's turn; its appearance works as a discursive anchor either way. Note that when

CHAPTER 5 A COGNITIVE LINGUISTIC ACCOUNT OF *I MEAN*   91

turn-taking occurs without a marker such as *I mean*, the entire utterance that cuts in conflates the function of both the anchor and the anchored structure. As will be described more extensively in the following section, when used to hold a turn, *I mean* no longer functions as an anchor, but simply as a parenthetical insertion.

5.4.3.4 Clause Internal *I mean* as a Parenthetical Insertion

Imo (2005) cited the following example of a turn-internal *I mean*:

(73)   a:nd sit over here and say it's NOT WRO:: *i mean* it's WRONG to
       FIGHT   (ibid. 7)

According to Imo (2005), in (73), the vowel "o" on the left next to *I mean* and the vowel "i" of *I mean* are *integrated seamlessly into the intonation contour* with the surrounding utterance (ibid. 7). That is, *I mean* does not compose a single IU but is integrated into the surrounding sounds, which runs counter to the description of clause-external anchors as *preposed to a finite clause and set off from the clause by "comma intonation"* (Langacker 2015). Therefore, *I mean* in the middle of a clause is outside the scope of the anchoring structure and cannot be accounted for by this notion because it has completely lost its status as anchor. Instead, this phenomenon might be ascribed to "parenthetical insertion," as proposed by Langacker (2009: 347). Langacker emphasized that parenthetical insertion must be examined in terms of not only processing time (T) but also phonological grouping (P). As shown in Figure 5.34, the parenthetical insertion of *I think* is not an interruption of time (Figure 5.34 (a)), but composes a phonological grouping independent of surrounding groupings (Figure 5.34 (b)).

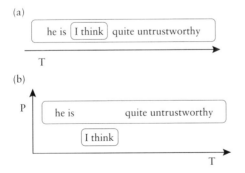

Figure 5.34: *I think* as a parenthetical insertion   (Ibid. 347)

The clause-initial *I mean*, which lost its status as anchor, can also be explained in terms of parenthetical insertion. In (73), therefore, *it's NOT WRO:: i mean* as a whole is phonologically inserted in the sequence *a:nd sit over here and say ... it's WRONG to FIGHT-*.

In section 5.4.3, the clausal positions of *I mean* are theoretically motivated by the notion of anchoring structure, which is based on discourse structure. Clause-initial *I mean* functions as an anchor; *I mean* as a matrix clause functions as part of the existential core, while at the effective and discursive level and partly at the speech management level, *I mean* as a whole functions as a discursive anchor. Clause-internal *I mean*, through which the speaker replaces information or holds a turn in the conversation, has lost its status as an anchor but forms another IU that is integrated with surrounding sounds, through a so-called parenthetical insertion.

5.5 Implications of the Cognitive Linguistic Account of Other Discourse Markers

I mean is defined as a marker that signals "intersubjective adjustment" and this adjustment is realized at various levels of discourse: the effective level (or what-is-said level), discursive level (or implicature level), speech management level (or turn level), and face level. The motivation for using *I mean* can be described as follows: to obey the offended maxims or save the threatened face, in a pragmatic account, and to adjust what the speaker and hearer pay attention to, in a cognitive linguistic account. One may doubt whether it is appropriate to refer to intersubjectivity when defining discourse markers because they are all used in communication and are intersubjective in nature, but we believe this is a mere first step and it is vital to compare discourse markers in terms of how the component meanings are reflected (cf. Schiffrin 1987), how their diachronic change proceeds (cf. Brinton 2008), and how their historical paths affect synchronic usages.

First, we compare *I mean* to other discourse markers based on this study. For the discourse markers *you know, well, like, yeah, actually, honestly*, which seem to be as highly functional and intersubjective as *I mean*, we will define why the speaker uses them. Next, the investigation shows the levels of discourse at which they function. It is easy to anticipate how *you know* works at the discursive, speech management, and face levels, but not at the effective level. While *I mean* has the power to profile the schematic relationship between propositions, *you know* does not because the speaker relies more on the hearer's understanding when using *you know* (cf. Tanaka and Ishizaki 1994: 14). *Like*, which has recently become notorious as the most frequent marker, appears to be similar to *I mean* in that it has various usages apart from that of its original meaning as filler (cf. Jucker and Smith 1998). According to Schourup (1985), *like* shows both the gap between what is said and what the speaker actually has in mind. The gap represented by *like* sounds similar to that of *I mean*, but these markers differ in that the speaker usually pays attention to what is said in the case of the former, whereas in the case of the latter, the speaker pays more attention to the hearer than in the case of the former.

In addition, meanings and usages of various discourse markers can be described as a network. While some markers profile elements in objective content, elements in the ground are foregrounded in the other markers. It is predictable that each meaning and usage overlaps and forms a complex network. Langacker (2008) notes that *because* has various usages that function at the effective, epistemic, and discursive levels and that overlap with *thus*. It is also interesting that the difference between *because* and *cos* in terms of phonological realization reflects their usages at the level of propositional content and implication (cf. Stenström 1998), but no consensus exists among researchers on the relationship between prosodic characteristics and the functions of discourse markers.

Overall, this study is merely a starting point for the construction of an entire system of discourse markers with a cognitive linguistics perspective. As a first step, we investigate the motivation for using other discourse markers and how these usages are related to each other. Next, we clarify how the usages of other markers can be mapped with relation to *I mean* and how they overlap.

5.6 Summary

The purpose of this chapter is to provide a unified theoretical account for the usages of *I mean* in terms of cognitive linguistics, based on Verhagen's (2007) notion of intersubjectivity and Langacker's (2001, 2008) account of CDS and anchoring structure. Because of the notion of intersubjectivity, the relationship between the usages can be explained as a process of subjectivity, and the difference between them can be explained as a profile shift from the elements of the object of conceptualization to those of the ground. While the details of the coordination of specific information cannot be described by pragmatic theories, such as Grice's Cooperative Principle and Politeness Theory, they can be in terms of what Verhagen illustrates as intersubjective coordination. However, attempts to explain all interpersonal usages as intersubjective coordination failed because the pragmatic notions of turn-taking and face-saving are beyond the scope of Verhagen's intersubjectivity. Instead, Langacker's cognitive model CDS that encompasses these pragmatic notions could be used to describe the cognitive process related to the usages of *I mean*, making it possible to describe all usages in a unified manner.

The discourse marker *I mean* is defined as a marker for intersubjective adjustment in this book. The term "adjustment" is used instead of "coordination" because the former has a wider scope over turn-taking and face-saving, similar to the way Fox Tree and Schrock (2002) used the term. Within the CDS model, *I mean* functions at the effective discursive, speech management, and face levels. As mentioned in Chapter 4, the motivation for using *I mean* involves the violation of Grice's Maxims and the threat to the hearer's face. Pragmatic theories, however, do not fully account for what is happening in the speaker's mind. The CDS analysis suggests an explanation for this matter: The speaker directs the hearer's attention to the relationship between elements of the propositional content at the effective level; he directs the hearer's attention to what he focuses on to achieve joint attention at the discursive level; he invites the hearer's attention to the schematic notion of turn to adjust its exchanges at the speech management level; and he directs his attention to the threatened face of the hearer and, subsequently, they jointly direct their attention to the speaker's attempt to redress the threat. Because the existing CDS is not sufficiently precise to describe the dynamic cognitive processes related to *I mean* at the discursive and face levels, we proposed a new version of CDS comprised of multiple phases.

The end of this chapter discussed the position of *I mean*. Although the matter of why so many instances of *I mean* appear in the clause- or turn-initial position has not been carefully examined in the previous studies, the model for anchoring structure provides a cognition-based explanation. It requires a reversal in thinking; when you define a linguistic element that often appears in a specific position in discourse, it becomes vulnerable to counterarguments to reasoning and tends to end up as circular reasoning instead. However, Langacker's (2009, 2015) proposed that the initial position, but not the linguistic element, serves a specific function. This function is called the anchor, and it functions as a reference point to help the hearer understand the following types of content: proposition, clause, or schematic process expressed by the existential core. *I mean* has a high frequency in the clause-initial position because the frame invoked by *I mean*, "what the speaker truly wants to direct hearer's attention to is going to follow," is compatible with its function of initial position, namely its function as an anchor, at different levels of discourse. The clause-medial *I mean* then no longer functions as an anchor, but rather as a parenthetical insertion.

Notes

1 The "onstage region" is metaphorical paraphrase of "immediate scope." While watching a play in the theater, we usually focus on someone or something spotlighted on the stage. When we express something, we also highlight an entity. According to Langacker (2009: 141), *an expression's immediate scope is defined as the general locus of viewing attention, those facets of the overall situation put "onstage" as being immediately relevant at a given level of organization for a particular purpose.*

2 The process of "objectification" is described as follows:
> ... Such a process may appropriately be characterized as one of objectification: initially, an expression does not profile any element of an object of conceptualization, but in the end it does. (Verhagen 2007: 73)

3 According to Langacker (2008), in (49d), *having the tickets for the game is the reason for asking the question* (ibid. 485). However, in terms of the purpose of the speaker using *because*, it seems more appropriate to explain *because* at Discursive Level as the reinforcement of the speaker's implication of "I want to do something with you" because any question does not necessarily function in the same way as *Are you busy tonight?* (e.g.,? *Are you hungry now, because I've got tickets to the game?*).

4 Elements composing the "(existential) core" are the ones pivotal to the "existence" of an event represented by a clause (Langacker 2015). *Its central members include the existential verb, the clausal subject, as well as indications of polarity and illocutionary force* (Langacker 2009: 246).

5 Langacker (2015: 20) notes that there is no clear boundary between the two anchors and that it is a matter of degree; among interclausal connections, *after* and *because*, tend to function descriptively, and *moreover* and *furthermore* tend to function discursively.

6 The aim of this study, however, is not to clarify the difference between *I think* and *I mean*, but the difference between the usages of *I mean*. The former issue will be discussed in another study.

7 The profile relationship in Figure 5.18 is similar to that of the usage of physical relationship (as in (49a)) of the connective *because* (cf. Verhagen 2005: 159). The construal configuration of this usage differs from the original usage and the usage at the what-is-said level in this respect, namely functioning to connect the two propositional contents. Onodera (2011), quoting Traugott (1995), noted that the speaker uses discourse markers to evaluate the relationship between the two propositional contents but not the way in which the speaker refers to the content.
> What DMs do is allow speakers to display their evaluation not of the content of what is said, but of the way it is put together, in other words, they do metatextual work.
> (Traugott 1995:6, quoted in Onodera 2011: 615)

8 Though Verhagen (2005, 2007) does not mention this clearly, from his descriptions of construal configurations, it seems reasonable to suppose that the profiled vertical line represents construal when either of the two conceptualizers in the ground is profiled, while it represents joint attention when both of them are profiled.

9 Although in some examples from BNC and COCA, the speaker's turn ends with *I mean*, this does not necessarily indicate that the following utterance is unexpected. In contrast to *you know*, which has the function of relinquishing a turn during conversation, *I mean* always evokes the anticipation of a following utterance. The following example represents the power of projection of a subsequent utterance by means of another speaker's utterance, namely, *You mean what?*

(74) She stammered and said, "Well, I ... ***I mean*** ..." "You mean what? That I don't

have as much money as you do?" (COCA)

10 The speaker's purpose of turn-taking is observed from his stammering *I'm like...* after *I mean*.
11 The following figure shows that the clause-initial *I mean* has superiority in numbers in PDE.

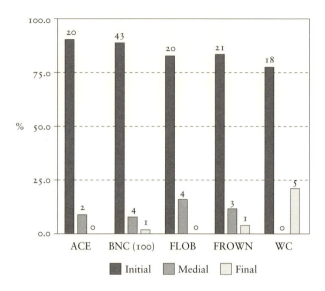

Figure 5.35: Positions of ***I mean*** (Brinton 2008: 119)

CHAPTER 6
I mean as a Marker of Intersubjective Adjustment

Previous studies have taken for granted that *I mean* is a marker of modification and have emphasized classifying and labeling its usages. Therefore, little work has been done on the background process underlying why speakers use *I mean*. For example, it makes no difference whether *I mean* is used to add a physical cause for the event represented in the preceding utterance, or to provide a reason for speech acts because both usages are labeled causal meaning or reason. The purpose of this study is to clarify the motivation for using *I mean* and to provide a theoretical background for the relationship between usages by means of descriptions of dynamic cognitive processes related to the uses of *I mean*.

Chapter 4 describes the motivation for using *I mean* as violation of Grice's Maxims or a threat to the hearer's face, and *I mean* demonstrates the speaker's will to follow the maxim or to save face. The former motivation is realized at two levels: the what-is-said level and the implicature level. For the latter motivation, the speaker uses *I mean* because he has threatened the hearer's face in the preceding discourse, and he therefore shows his will to redress the threat to the hearer's face in the discourse that follows. This lets speaker correct information without admitting his mistake and apology, and this may be ascribed to the speaker's attempt to save either his own positive face or the hearer's positive face. Because of pragmatic theories, such as Grice's Conversational Principle and Politeness Theory, the motivations for using *I mean* have a direct relationship to what-is-said, implicature, and face-threatening. There can be no doubt that the participants follow Grice's CP (cf. Tomasello 2008), since the speaker uses *I mean* to highlight the violation of a maxim and his intention to be cooperative. However, pragmatic theories do not explain the process of the speaker's anticipation of what the hearer thinks, which is observed in the usage at the implicature level. In addition, the pragmatic account of *I mean* uses different theories for different usages, and this ad-hoc manner of explanation does not help us to grasp what *I mean* is.

Chapter 5 uses a cognitive linguistic account to address the abovementioned problem and provide the theoretical background for the motivation for using *I mean* in a unified manner. Specifically, the concept of intersubjectivity proposed by Verhagen (2007) and the cognitive discourse model (CDS) developed by Langacker (2001, 2008) show that the speaker's motivation can be attributed to basic human abilities, such as reference point, intersubjectivity, and specificity. Either at the effective level or discursive level, the speaker uses *I mean* to direct the hearer's attention to the speaker's object of focus. This relies on the speaker's ability to take another person's perspective, namely intersubjectivity. However, in reality, this process is more complicated because what the speaker and hearer pay attention to differ in the preceding utterance, and that difference is the very motivation for using *I mean*. There are several steps in the cognitive process related to *I mean* at the discursive level. However, the existing CDS cannot account for the process. For this reason, we propose a new version of CDS comprising several phases to reflect the dynamicity of the process in its description. For the speech management level and face level, the processes of turn-taking and face-saving are realized in the interaction between the speaker and the hearer of the ground and in the channel of conceptualization that differs from the level of objective content, respectively. The usages of *I mean* vary in that their conceptualization can occur at the level of objective content, speech acts or implicatures, abstract turn, and social face. Nevertheless, their conceptualizations differ in the degree of specificity (or schematicity), and they all share the fact that the speaker's construals are reflected in the cognitive process related to *I mean*.

The motivation for the use of *I mean* and the relationship between the usages were then described in a single cognitive linguistic account based on Langacker's (2001, 2008) CDS model. In this CG account, *I mean* is defined as a marker of intersubjective adjustment, and it functions to adjust the relationship between elements of the propositional content, implicature, turn, and face at the four different levels of discourse. The motivation for using *I mean* can be explained simply and schematically as seeking joint attention between the speaker and hearer. In addition, the positions of *I mean* are theoretically motivated by Langacker's (2001, 2009) model of anchoring structure: Clause-initial *I mean* functions as an anchor, and clause-internal *I mean* as functions as a parenthetical insertion.

References

Akimoto, Minoji (2002) *Bunpooka to Idiomuka (Grammaticalization and Idiomatization)*, Hituzi Shobo Publishing, Tokyo.

Akimoto, Minoji (2010) "Comment Clause towa (What are comment clauses?)," *Comment Clause no Shiteki Kenkyuu: Sono Kinou to Hattatsu (Historical Study on Comment Clause: Its Functions and Develpoments)*," ed. by Minoji Akimoto, 1–28, Eichousha Phoenix, Tokyo.

Biber et al. (1999) *Longman Grammar of Spoken and Written English*, Longman, London.

Brinton, Laurel J. (2008) *The Comment Clause in English*, Cambridge University Press, Cambridge.

Brown, Penelope and Stephen C. Levinson (1987) *Politeness: Some Universal in Language Usage*, Cambridge University Press, Cambridge.

Dehé, Nicole and Anne Wichmann (2010) "The Multifunctionality of Epistemic Parentheticals in Discourse: Prosodic Cues to the Semantic-pragmatic Boundary," *Functions of Language* 17(1), 1–28.

Diessel, Holger and Michael Tomasello (2001) "The Acquisition of Finite Complement Clauses in English: A Corpus Based Analysis," *Cognitive Linguistics* 12, 97–141.

Erman, Britt (1987) *Pragmatic Expressions in English: A Study of 'You know,' 'You see' and 'I mean' in Face-to-Face Conversation*, Almqvist and Wiksell, Stockholm.

Fauconnier, Gilles (1994) *Mental Spaces*, Cambridge University Press, New York.

Finell, Anne (1992) "The Repertoire of Topic Changers in Personal, Intimate Letters: A Diachronic Study of Osborne and Woolf," *History of Englishes: New Methods and Interpretations in Historical Linguistics*, ed. by Matti Rissanen et al, 720–735.

Fischer, Rotraut (1992) "Disfluenz als kontextualisierungshinweis in telefonischen Beratungsgesprächen im Rundfunk," *KontRi* 23, Konstanz.

Fox Tree, Jean E. and Josef C. Schrock (2002) "Basic Meanings of *You Know* and *I Mean*," *Journal of Pragmatics* 34, 727–747.

Fukuhara, Yuichi (2010) "Face-Work to Discourse Marker no Youhou Kakuchou:

Bunmatsu Hyogen *Zyan* no Bunseki wo Rei ni Shite (Face-Work and Functional Extension of Discourse Markers: Analysis of Sentence-final Expression 'Zyan')," *Human Communication Studies* 38, 159-172.

Goldberg, Adele E (2006) *Constructions at work: the nature of generalization in language*, Oxford University Press, Oxford.

Grice, Paul H. (1975) "Logic and Conversation," *Syntax and semantics: Speech acts*, ed. by Cole Peter and Morgan, Jerry L., 41-58, Academic Press, New York.

Grice, Paul H. (1989) *Studies in the Way of Words*, Harvard University Press, Cambridge, MA.

Halliday, M. A. K. and Ruqayia Hasan (1976) *Cohesion in English*, Longman, London.

Hirose, Kozo and Fumiko Matsuo (2015) "Appendix I: A. Danwa Hyoushiki Kenkyuu no Ayumi (Appendix I: A. Progress in Discourse Marker Studies)," *Eigo Danwa Hyoushiki Youhou Jiten (A Dictionary of Discourse Markers in English)*, ed. by Fumiko Matsuo, Kozo Hirose, and Mayumi Nishikawa, 321-332, Kenkyusha, Tokyo.

Hopper, Paul J. and Elizabeth Closs Traugott (^{1}1993. ^{2}2003) *Grammaticalization*, 1st edn, 2nd edn, (Cambridge Textbooks in Linguisctics,) Cambridge University Press, Cambridge.

Horn, Laurence (2009) "Wj-40: Implicature, Truth and Meaning," *International Review of Pragmatics* 1 (1), 3-34.

Huang, Yan (2014) *Pragmatics Second Edition*, Oxford University Press, Oxford.

Imo, Wolfgang (2005) "A Construction Grammar Approach to the Phrase *I mean* in Spoken English," InList (Interaction and Linguistic Structure) 42, 1-37.

Itkonen Esa (2008) "The Central Role of Normativity in Language and Linguistics," *The Shared Mind: Perspectives on Intersubjectivity*, ed. by Jordan Zlatev et al., 307-331, John Benjamins Publishing Company, Amsterdam/Philadelphia.

Jucker, Andreas H. and Sara W. Smith (1998) "*And people just like 'wow'* Discourse Markers as Negotiating Strategies," *Discourse Markers: Description and Theory*, ed. by Jucker, Andreas H. and Yael Ziv, 171-201, John Benjamins, Amsterdam.

Kobayashi, Takashi (2013) "America-jin Daigakusei no Danwa Hyoushiki Shiyou Keikou: Tufts Daigaku no Gakusei eno Chousa kara (The Tendency of Use of Discourse Markers among American University Students: Based on the Speech Data From Tufts University Students)," *Kanazawa Cultural Resource Studies* 12, 158-164, Kanazawa University.

Kobayashi, Takashi (2016) "CDS no Shatei: Danwa Hyoushiki *I mean* no Atarashii Rei karano Kenshou (The Scope of CDS: A Study from the New Usages of the Discourse Marker *I mean*)," *Proceedings of the 18th Conference of the Pragmatics Society of Japan*, 41-48.

Langacker, Ronald W. (1991) *Foundations of Cognitive Grammar* vol. 2, *Descriptive Application*, Stanford University Press, Stanford.

Langacker, Ronald W. (1993) "Reference-Point Constructions," *Cognitive Linguistics* 4, 1–38.
Langacker, Ronald W. (1999) *Grammar and Conceptualization*, Mouton de gruyter,
Langacker, Ronald W. (2001) "Discourse in Cognitive Grammar," *Cognitive Linguistics* 12 (2), 143–188.
Langacker, Ronald W. (2008) *Cognitive Grammar: A Basic Introduction*, Oxford University Press, New York.
Langacker, Ronald W. (2009) *Investigations in Cognitive Grammar*. Mouton de Gruyter, New York.
Langacker, Ronald W. (2015) "How to Build an English Clause," *Journal of Foreign Language Teaching and Applied Linguistics* 2 (2). doi: 10.14706/JFLTAL15121, (cited 2018-1-25).
Lewis, David (1969) *Convention: A Philosophical Study*, Harvard University Press, Cambridge, MA.
Leech, Geoffrey (1983) *Principles of Pragmatics*, Longman, New York.
Lenk, Uta (1998) *Marking Discourse Coherence: Functions of Discourse Markers in Spoken English*, Gunter Narr Verlag, Tübingen.
Levinson, Stephen C. (1983) *Pragmatics*, Cambridge University Press, Cambridge.
Levinson, Stephen C. (2000) *Presumptive Meanings: The Theory of Generalized Conversational Implicature*, MIT Press, Cambridge, Mass.
Markkanen, Raija (1985) "English Parenthetical Clauses of the Type 'I believe/you know' and their Finnish Equivalents," *Cross-Linguistics Studies in Pragmatics (Jyväskylä Cross-Language Studies* 11), 45–63, Dept. of English, University of Jyväskylä, Jyväskylä.
Matsui, Nobuyoshi (2009) "*I mean* no Kinouteki Tokuchou ni Kansuru Ichikousatsu (A Study on the Functional Properties of *I mean*)," *Bulletin of Maizuru National College of Technology* No.44, 53–61, Maizuru National College of Technology.
Muzikant, Mojmír (2007) "Comment Clauses and their Role in Spoken English," *Master Thesis*, Masaryk University, Brno, Czech Republic.
Ogden, C. K. and I. A. Richards (1923) *The Meaning of meaning: A Study of the Influence of Language upon Thought and of the Science Symbolism*, Routledge & Kegan Paul Ltd, London.
Onodera, Noriko O. (2011) "The Grammaticalization of Discourse Markers", *The Oxford Handbook of Grammaticalization*, ed. by Heiko Narrog and Berned Heine, 614–624, Oxford University Press, Oxford.
Quirk, Randolph, Sidney Greenbaum, Geoffrey Leech, and Jan Svartvik (1985) *A Comprehensive Grammar of the English Language*, Longman, London.
Sacks, H., Schegloff, E. A., and Jefferson, G. (1974) "A Simplest Systematics for the Organization of Turn-taking for Conversation," *Language*, 50 (4), 696–735.
Sakita, Tomoko (2010) "Ninchi to Danwa・Jouhou (Cognition and Discourse・Information)," *Gengo Unyou no Dynamism: Ninchigoyouron no Approach, Kouza*

Ninchigengogaku no Frontier vol. 4 *(Dynamism in language use: Cognitive Pragmatic Approach, Frontier in Cognitive Linguistics* vol.4*)*, ed. by Masaaki Yamanashi, 1-12, Kenkyusha, Tokyo.

Sawada, Harumi (2001) "Suii (Implicature)," *Nyuumon Goyouron Kenkyu: Riron to Ouyou (An Intorduction to Pragmatic Study: Theory and Application)*, ed. by Tamotsu Koizumi, 35-63, Kenkyusha, Tokyo.

Saul, Jennifer M. (2002) "What Is Said and Psychological Reality: Grice's Project and Relevance Theorists' Criticisms," *Linguistics and Philosophy* 25, 347-372, Kluwer Academic Publishers, Netherlands.

Schiffrin, Deborah (1987) *Discourse Markers*, Cambridge University Press, Cambridge.

Schourup, Lawrence C. (1985) *Common Discourse Particles in English Conversation: like, well, y'know*, Academic Press, New York.

Schourup, Lawrence C. (1999) "Discourse Markers", *Lingua* 107, 227-265.

Sperber, Dan and Deirdre Wilson (1986) *Relevance: communication and cognition*, Harvard University Press, Cambridge, Mass.

Stenström, Anna-Brita (1994) *An Introduction to Spoken Interaction*, Longman, London.

Stenström, Anna-Brita (1995) "Some Remarks on Comment Clauses," *The Verb in Contemporary English*, ed. by Bas Aarts and Charles F. Meyer, 290-301, Cambridge University Press, Cambridge.

Stenström, Anna-Brita (1998) "From Sentence to Discourse: Cos (because) in Teenage Talk," *Discourse Markers: Description and Theory*, ed. by Jucker, Andreas H. and Yael Ziv, 127-146, John Benjamins, Amsterdam.

Sweetser, Eve E. (1990) *From Etymology to Pragmatics: Metaphorical and Cultural Aspects of Semantic Structure*, Cambridge University Press, Cambridge.

Takahara, Osamu, Takuo Hayashi, and Reiko Hayashi (2002) *Pragmatics no Tenkai (Pragmatics)*, Keiso Shobo, Tokyo.

Tanaka, Shigenori and Shun Ishizaki (1994) "Nichijou Gengo ni Okeru Imi no Seisei: You Know to I Mean no Yakuwari (Meaning Making in Conversational Language: The Roles of *You Know* and *I Mean*)," *IPSJ SIG Technical Report* 28, 9-16.

Tomasello, Michael (2008) *Origins of Human Communication*, MIT Press.

Traugott, Elizabeth C. (1995) "The Role of Discourse Markers in a Theory of Grammaticalization," paper presented at the 12th International Conference on Historical Linguistics Manchester, August.

Traugott, Elizabeth C. and Richard B. Dasher (2002) *Regularity in Semantic Change (Cambridge Studies in Linguistics* 96), Cambridge University Press, Cambridge.

Verhagen, Arie (2005) *Constructions of Intersubjectivity: Discourse, Syntax, and Cognition*, Oxford University Press, Oxford.

Verhagen, Arie (2007) "Construal and Perspectualization," *The Oxford Handbook of Cognitive Linguistics*, ed. by Dirk Geeraerts and Hubert Cuyckens, 48-81, Oxford University Press, Oxford.

Yamanashi, Masaaki (2001) "Ninchigoyouron (Cognitive Pragmatics)," *Nyuumon Goyouron Kenkyu: Riron to Ouyou (An Intorduction to Pragmatic Study: Theory and Application)*, ed. by Tamotsu Koizumi, 179-194, Kenkyusha, Tokyo.

Index

A
adjustment   24, 92
anchor   66

B
because   65

C
channels   62
cognitive salience   87
conceptualization   54
conceptualizer   54
Cooperative Principle   36
coordination relationship   59
CRMTP   11

D
discourse markers   7
dynamic cognitive process   82

E
(existential) core   66

F
face   44

G
gradation   54
(Grice's) maxims   36
ground   57

I
I think   60
implicature   36
interaction   77
intersubjectivity   72, 81
intonation units (IUs)   30
invited inference   29

J
joint attention   58

L
levels   64
levels of discourse   92
levels of knowledge   84
like   13, 92

M
mental space   72

N
negative politeness   45
network   28

P
parenthetical insertion   91
perspective   56
phases   82
politeness   19, 44
positive politeness   45
profile   55

R
result phase   86

S
specificity   56
subjectification   60

T
tags   90

U
unidirectionality   17
usage event   61

V
viewing frame   61

W
what is said   36

小林隆（こばやし たかし）

略歴
2010年金沢大学文学部卒業。
2016年金沢大学大学院人間社会環境研究科博士後期課程修了。
現在、石川工業高等専門学校一般教育科講師。

Takashi Kobayashi received Ph.D. degree from Kanazawa University, Japan in 2016. He is currently an associate professor in Institute of Technology, Ishikawa College.

主な論文
- "A Pragmatic and Cognitive Approach to the Usage of *I mean*," *Human and Socio-Environmental Studies* 25. (2013)
- 「談話標識 *I mean* の使用原理についての認知言語学的考察」『日本認知言語学会論文集』第14巻（2014）
- 「指示代名詞 *that* の用法に関する認知語用論的考察」『日本認知言語学会論文集』第17巻（2017）

Hituzi Linguistics in English No.27
I mean as a Marker of Intersubjective Adjustment
A Cognitive Linguistic Approach

発行	2018年2月16日 初版1刷
定価	8500円＋税
著者	©小林隆
発行者	松本功
ブックデザイン	白井敬尚形成事務所
印刷所	株式会社 ディグ
製本所	株式会社 星共社
発行所	株式会社 ひつじ書房

〒112-0011 東京都文京区千石2-1-2 大和ビル2F
Tel: 03-5319-4916
Fax: 03-5319-4917
郵便振替 00120-8-142852
toiawase@hituzi.co.jp
http://www.hituzi.co.jp/
ISBN978-4-89476-902-1

造本には充分注意しておりますが、落丁・乱丁などがございましたら、小社かお買上げ書店にておとりかえいたします。ご意見、ご感想など、小社までお寄せ下されば幸いです。

刊行のご案内

認知言語学論考

認知言語学論考　No.11
山梨正明他 編　定価 9,800 円 + 税
執筆者：菊田千春、黒滝真理子、中野研一郎、今井新悟、名塩征史、寺西隆弘、大西美穂、徳山聖美、金光成、山本幸一

認知言語学論考　No.12
山梨正明他 編　定価 9,800 円 + 税
執筆者：黒田一平、小松原哲太、加藤祥、岡本雅史、荒牧英治、小川典子、野澤元、田口慎也、今井隆夫、甲田直美、和田尚明、田村敏広、土屋智行、年岡智見

認知言語学論考　No.13
山梨正明他 編　定価 9,800 円 + 税
執筆者：山梨正明、町田章、籾山洋介、岡田禎之、李在鎬、和佐敦子、澤田淳、杉山さやか、呂佳蓉、伊藤薫

刊行のご案内

ファンダメンタル英語学　改訂版
中島平三 著　定価 1,400 円＋税

ファンダメンタル認知言語学
野村益寛 著　定価 1,600 円＋税

刊行のご案内

発話のはじめと終わり
語用論的調節のなされる場所
小野寺典子 編　定価 3,800 円＋税

神奈川大学言語学研究叢書　7
動詞の意味拡張における方向性
着点動作主動詞の認知言語学的研究
夏海燕 著　定価 4,800 円＋税

刊行のご案内

ひつじ研究叢書（言語編）

第143巻 相互行為における指示表現
須賀あゆみ 著　定価6,400円+税

第151巻 多人数会話におけるジェスチャーの同期
「同じ」を目指そうとするやりとりの会話分析
城綾実 著　定価5,800円+税

第152巻 日本語語彙的複合動詞の意味と体系
コンストラクション形態論とフレーム意味論
陳奕廷・松本曜 著　定価8,500円+税

刊行のご案内

英語コーパス研究シリーズ
堀正広・赤野一郎監修　定価 各3,200円＋税

第1巻　コーパスと英語研究（近刊）
第2巻　コーパスと英語教育
第3巻　コーパスと辞書（近刊）
第4巻　コーパスと英文法・語法
第5巻　コーパスと英語文体
第6巻　コーパスと英語史（近刊）
第7巻　コーパスと多様な関連領域

刊行のご案内

Hituzi Language Studies

No. 1 Relational Practice in Meeting Discourse in
New Zealand and Japan
村田和代 著　定価 6,000 円 + 税

No. 2 Style and Creativity
Towards a Theory of Creative Stylistics
斎藤兆史 著　定価 7,500 円 + 税

No. 3 Rhetorical Questions
A Relevance-Theoretic Approach to Interrogative Utterances in English
and Japanese
後藤リサ 著　定価 10,000 円 + 税

刊行のご案内

Hituzi Linguistics in English

No. 24 Metaphor of Emotions in English
With Special Reference to the Natural World and the Animal Kingdom as Their Source Domains
大森文子 著　定価 9,500 円＋税

No. 25 A Comparative Study of Compound Words
向井真樹子 著　定価 13,000 円＋税

No. 26 Grammatical Variation of Pronouns in Nineteenth-Century English Novels
中山匡美 著　定価 12,000 円＋税